BEHAVIOURAL SCIENCE FOR MARKETING AND BUSINESS STUDENTS

SECOND EDITION

Joseph MacDonagh,
Carol Linehan,
Rebecca Weldridge

GILL & MACMILLAN

Gill & Macmillan Ltd
Hume Avenue
Park West
Dublin 12
with associated companies throughout the world
www.gillmacmillan.ie

Index compiled by Grainne Farren
Print origination in Ireland by Linda Kelly

This book is typeset in Palantino 11pt on 13.5pt.

The paper used in this book comes from the wood pulp of managed forests. For every tree felled, at least one tree is planted, thereby renewing natural resources.

CONTENTS

FOREWORD TO THE FIRST EDITION

As psychologists lecturing in the areas of management and marketing, we became acutely aware of the need for a textbook that dealt with the basic behavioural science concepts and theories in a straightforward and jargon-free way. This book caters for students of business courses (whether sales, advertising, marketing or management) and of other non-psychology subjects involving aspects of human behaviour.

We have counteracted the tendency in many textbooks used in Irish courses to focus exclusively on American or British examples. As well as giving the book a better balance, we have made sure that the book is easily accessible for student learning and reference. Each chapter begins with learning objectives, has clearly defined section headings, contains summaries in point form and ends with possible exam questions (some drawn from professional bodies' past papers).

We believe we have explained simply and accurately the theories of behavioural sciences.

Joseph MacDonagh, M.A.
Business School
RTC Tallaght
Dublin

Rebecca Weldridge, M.A.
School of Business & Marketing
College of Marketing and
 Design
Dublin

FOREWORD TO THE SECOND EDITION

With this second edition of *Behavioural Science* we hope to build on the aims of the first, explaining the concepts of behavioural science in an accessible way with examples from business areas such as management, marketing, sales and advertising. For this latest edition, we have listened closely to the feedback from students, reviewers and colleagues.

The main difference from when we first published *Behavioural Science* in 1994 is that the world, and Ireland in particular, is a very different place. As we describe in the chapter on Irish social change, Ireland is significantly more affluent and diverse than it was, and its key demographics have changed substantially.

Though the fundamentals of behavioural science have not changed in this time, there is scarcely an area where technology—whether it be mobile phones, computers or the Internet—is not used today. For this reason, we have tried to exemplify behavioural science principles with reference to these areas.

You will see as well that there is a new co-author, Carol Linehan. Rebecca Weldridge did not take part in the writing of this new edition, but we are grateful to her for all the work she put into the first edition. Without her input, it would not have been what it was.

We hope you enjoy this latest edition and that it helps you both personally and professionally.

Joseph MacDonagh,
 M.A. Reg. Psychol.
Department of Management
Institute of Technology, Tallaght
Dublin

Carol Linehan, PhD.
Department of Management
 and Marketing
University College Cork

INTRODUCTION

Behavioural science is the study of people and their behaviour. We review the principles of the science, with each chapter addressing a different issue, as follows:

Chapter 1 is a general **introductory section** to explain what behavioural science is, how it tries to attain the goals of a science and how it uses scientific methodology to collect and collate data in order to produce objective and scientific results.

Chapter 2 examines the issue of **perception,** how we see the world around us. As each of us is unique, our outlooks differ. We investigate the way in which processes of perceptual selection and organisation contribute to this difference. Lastly, we discuss social perception and how we view and relate to other people.

Chapter 3 concentrates on theories of **learning and memory.** We focus on two different theories. One—the behaviourist approach—proposes that learning behaviour is merely a case of conditioning. The other—the cognitive approach—claims that learning involves higher mental processes, such as insight and understanding. This chapter also examines memory, how we remember, how we forget and what mechanisms we use to memorise material.

Chapter 4 explores a number of **motivational theories.** We investigate theorists such as Abraham Maslow, David C. McClelland and others whose works are used in today's business world. The understanding of motivation is as important for those who manage as those who are managed.

Chapter 5 identifies the complex components and functions of **attitudes.** We look at how people acquire attitudes, how their attitudes affect behaviour and how they change. We examine a number of attitudinal theories and present their applications within both marketing and organisational spheres.

Chapter 6 discusses four approaches to **personality** theory, ranging from the psychoanalytic approach (Sigmund Freud and Carl Gustav

Jung) to the humanistic (Carl Rogers) and trait (Raymond Cattell) approaches.

Chapter 7 sees a slight change in orientation from the individual to **the group**. This chapter examines the make-up, development and functions of groups. The impact of group influence on individual behaviour is also reviewed.

Chapter 8 focusses on **organisational life;** how organisations are structured, their approach to technology and recruitment and employee-employer relationships.

Chapter 9 looks at the concepts of **culture and society,** and the influence of both on human behaviour. As the three are inextricably linked, it is impossible to study human behaviour without this broad societal perspective.

Chapter 10 looks at the dramatic changes in **Irish society** over the past fifty years in terms of social and economic demographics. We also discuss the major trends in Irish society, and the way in which primary influences in Irish society still exert a strong 'pull' on our consciousness. This chapter details some of the reasons for the social and economic changes which have contributed to relative Irish affluence towards the end of the twentieth, and the start of the twenty-first, century.

Chapter 1

Behavioural Science

Whatever contributes to a knowledge of human activity,
is an admissable method to science.

Gordon W. Allport (1947)

1

Behavioural Science

Learning objectives

After studying this chapter, you should be able to:

1. *Understand the discipline of behavioural science and its applications in the real world.*

2. *Identify the problems of behavioural science in claiming to be a science.*

3. *Understand the ways in which behavioural scientists apply systematic analysis to the work they do.*

4. *Discuss the three basic research methodologies.*

5. *Summarise the scales of measurement used in behavioural science.*

1.1 INTRODUCTION

We examine here the origin, nature and applications of behavioural science, and ask:

(a)   Why do we study behavioural science?

(b)   What does it involve?

(c)   How do we study it?

In the book we have used examples from business, marketing and everyday life to show that the theories of behavioural science are clearly defined and applicable in all three areas.

1.2 WHY DO WE STUDY BEHAVIOURAL SCIENCE?

Marketers need a comprehensive and reliable knowledge of behavioural science to acquire insights into consumer behaviour. As noted by consumer behaviour theorist Chisnall (1985) 'buying behaviour should take account of the structure of society and the interactions of individuals within the various groups and subgroups … cultural beliefs, values …'

Consumerism is an interactive variable in the overall pattern of people's behaviour. For example, food and clothing often have social rather than solely functional values. Food can be used to enhance prestige; clothing can express status and personality. The growth and marketing of desirable brands in the clothing sector highlights how important psychological rather than functional factors can be in shaping consumer behaviour.

Often used by the marketing industry, **augmented product or service** is a concept that recognises buyer behaviour as a complex, interactive dynamic comprising many psychological, social and cultural factors, such as perceptions, motivations and attitudes. In today's world, it is necessary for marketers to understand the importance of the many factors affecting behaviour. The emphasis on consumer satisfaction is as much psychological as it is physical.

From an organisational perspective, behavioural science principles are of tremendous importance, as organisations consist of people and their often complex behaviours. Knowledge of this science may help management to:

(a)   Understand how employee attitudes and motivations affect interaction within the work place.

(b)   Understand the importance of psychological and social influences on employee performance levels.

(c)   Understand the need for specific interpersonal skills in the appraisal of staff or other communications with them.

Ineffective management leads to organisational mediocrity and perhaps failure. Effective management, incorporating behavioural science principles, helps an organisation to function at its optimum level.

Human behaviour does not occur in a vacuum. The causes of our behaviour are a combination of individual and social factors. As society becomes increasingly complex, the need to understand behavioural principles becomes more apparent. Unless we learn why people behave as they do, we cannot hope to understand them. By nature we are curious, not only about ourselves but also about our fellow beings. We are avid people-watchers; their behaviour perplexes and fascinates us. In the following chapters we try to identify some of the causes of human behaviour.

1.3 WHAT IS BEHAVIOURAL SCIENCE?

Behavioural science is a collective noun covering disciplines such as psychology, sociology, economics and anthropology. These are four distinct topics in their own right, yet complementary to the study of human behaviour.

Psychology studies human and animal behaviour with the ultimate goal of gathering knowledge for the benefit of humanity. It seeks to determine the causes of behaviour: the motives and attitudes and how individuals learn and modify responses to their environment. Psychologist William James (1890) defined psychology as the 'science of mental life'.

Sociology studies social structures, trends and the collective behaviour of individuals in groups. Of particular interest is the social influence of a group over individuals in terms of norms, status and power.

Anthropology examines the cultural determinants of human behaviour, focussing particularly on the demands of society that shape individual and group behaviour.

Economics studies the interaction of production, exchange and consumption of goods and services.

We focus mainly on the first discipline, psychology, in order to understand how and why individuals relate to each other and their environment. We borrow from sociology and anthropology where those disciplines enhance our understanding of the collective nature of people in terms of cultural and social influences, and we use some economic data in analysing the changes in Irish society over the last forty years or so.

Before proceeding further we must define some important concepts and terms integral to behavioural science.

Variable
The concept of a **variable** is central to the discipline of behavioural science. It means any entity that can vary. Behavioural science recognises two variables.

(a) **Independent variables** are the suspected causes of behaviour in an experiment.

(b) **Dependent variables** reveal the effects of the independent variables.

For example, one might study the effects of an in-store promotion campaign (independent variable) on sales of a particular product (dependent variable). These are discussed further later in the chapter.

Quantitative and qualitative research

Most behavioural research is quantitative: we observe a variable and then quantify or measure it. Qualitative research is more concerned with how people make sense of their world. It involves studying how people act in, and account for, meaningful situations.

As a broad contrast, consider the different use of questionnaires in quantitative and qualitative research. Quantitative research tends to ask subjects to complete questionnaires with **closed** questions and to respond yes or no (for example 'Do you think there is too much unemployment in the country?'). Such responses are then easily quantified and analysed.

In qualitative research respondents tend to be asked **open** questions that require an answer eliciting richer accounts or opinions (for example 'Why do you think unemployment is so high?'). Quantitative research measures the extent or degree of behaviour, while qualitative research examines the meanings of particular events for people.

Sampling

One must recognise the statistical notion of a **sample** drawn from a test population. Francis (1988) notes:

> In practice, most of the information obtained by organisations about any population will come from examining a small, representative subset of the population. This is called a sample. For example (a) a company might examine one in every twenty of their invoices for a month to determine the average amount of a customer order; (b) a newspaper might commission a research company to ask 1,000 potential voters their opinions on a forthcoming election. The information gathered from a sample (i.e. measurements, facts and/or opinions) will normally give a good indication of the measurements, facts and/or opinions of the population from which it was drawn.

The more representative the sample and the closer in size it is to the population, the more accurate it is likely to be. This introduces the notion of validity, examined later in the chapter.

1.3.1 Natural science vs. behavioural science

As noted by the psychologist E.G. Boring (Schultz, 1982) the application of the scientific method to the study of the mind is the greatest event in the history of psychology. If behavioural scientists believe scientific methodology is the only way of objectively researching and understanding human behaviour, they must systematically study behaviour using the principles and methods of scientific research.

Science is often thought of as a body of knowledge that is more objective than non-scientific forms of knowing. Natural sciences such as chemistry, physics and biology are relatively easy to study by measurement and control, with causal relationships being observed through experimentation and hypothesis (proposition) testing.

Science is a discipline dedicated to objectivity and evaluation. It has four goals:

Description: This involves the labelling, defining and classifying of objects, events, situations, and observable relationships between these.

Understanding: In some cases, this involves developing a theory to describe adequately the relationships between variables in a particular setting. In other cases, attempts are made to discover what causes a particular effect between variables.

Prediction: Accurate prediction (a) has practical value, and (b) gives a test of understanding.

Control: Control over the method of inquiry is necessary, particularly:

(a) Events that take place in the experiment.
(b) Extraneous variables (factors not being specifically researched) that could contaminate results.
(c) When and how behaviours under study will be measured.

The goals of science are complementary. Description opens doors to understanding, while prediction and control index the accuracy of our understanding. For example, let us assume that someone observes a change in worker productivity in the presence of music. A scientific study of this observation would begin with a description of the phenomenon, that worker productivity changes with the presence of background music.

To understand why this might happen a researcher begins to develop a theory, for example that music increases workers' levels of perceptual arousal and so contributes to increasing productivity in certain types of tasks. Variable A (presence of music) and Variable B (levels of productivity) would then have to be further defined: for example, what type of music is played, for how long, at what decibel level, etc. The type of work task would also need to be further specified; is it manual, repetitive, does it involve problem-solving, etc.

Once these variables have been defined, the researcher could design an experiment to test his/her predictions about the effect of music on productivity. In carrying out this experiment, control would have to be exercised to make sure that what is being tested is the relationship between Variable A and B and not interference from some other variable, such as taking a rest break. The following section takes you through the process of implementing a behavioural study step by step.

1.4 HOW DO WE STUDY BEHAVIOURAL SCIENCE?

If behavioural science wishes to call itself a science, how does it:

(a) Attain the goals of a science?

(b) Construct a systematic method of inquiry?

1.4.1 Forming the research question

Behavioural scientists have to describe and explain real-life responses by examining actual events. This involves testing their data against reality. They must map out a sequence of activities that meets the requirements of a scientific investigation. It can be summarised as follows:

Step 1: **Formulate the question** to be asked—what is to be studied? In our earlier example a suitable question might be 'Does the presence of background music increase worker productivity on manual tasks?'

Step 2: **Operationalise the question** by translating it into an appropriate research design—decide on the most appropriate manner of investigation. To study our question on music and productivity we would need to define the variables, for example defining music as classical, country or garage, played at 'X' decibel level. Productivity could be defined as the number of units (widgets) produced, the speed of production, or the number of mistakes avoided.

Step 3: **Measure the behaviour** of interest—observation of research participants under specific conditions and conversion of responses into data. In our example we might count the number of widgets produced across two shifts, one with music and the other without music.

Step 4: **Extract relationships** from data through the use of logic and statistics—control and measurement being vital for reliability. We could carry out tests on the data to see if there was a significant difference between the number of widgets produced with and without music.

Step 5: **Interpret relationships** with due consideration for theoretical implications. Having analysed our data and come up with results, we would interpret these results to see what the experiment tells us about the effect of music on productivity.

Step 6: Decide whether the research design used and the conclusions reached are **generalisable and repeatable**. In the case of our hypothetical experiment we would need to consider, for example, whether various types of music would have different effects on productivity.

One of the major concerns of research is how to operationalise the research question: in other words, how to decide on the best methodology. The research design is selected on three criteria:

(a) Nature of the question: Is it easily operationalised?

(b) Practical considerations: What will the problems be?

(c) Purpose of the study: Will the design disclose the type of information required?

1.4.2 Methodologies

Research methods involve processes of asking questions, observing behaviours, or intervening in situations. Three basic research methods are used in behavioural science. No one method is sufficient for researching all psychological topics; often a mixture of methods offers the best solution.

Methods differ from one another in the degree to which researchers intervene and change the environment of participants. One of the major research objectives is to control variables that bear on internal validity (see section 1.4.3).

The most common research methods are:

Inquiry methods

These methods hinge on 'asking' participants about their experiences. This could involve surveys, interviews, focus groups or case studies. Such methods can be loosely structured as in an informal interview or quite tightly structured as in a closed-ended survey.

Since surveys are commonly used in a marketing context we will expand on that particular method. Surveys tend to be conducted:

(a) By definition of population and variables of study, e.g. surveying women (population) on their choice of perfume (variable).

(b) By drawing a representative sample of people from the defined population, e.g. selecting a balanced number from various areas, ages and occupations.

(c) By measuring the target variables in the sample, e.g. how many women actually buy the perfume.

(d) On the basis of the sample variables, attempting general statements about the original population's variable, e.g. the amount of perfume purchased gives an idea of how popular it is with women generally.

Researcher intervention is necessary but control is quite low, especially in the case of postal surveys.

Systematic observation

This develops an accurate description of the behaviours and relationships of people who are involved in the activity of interest, e.g. work activity. This design generally involves the least researcher intervention, for example observing subjects through a two-way mirror or while engaged in their work activity.

As with inquiry methods, observations can vary in their degree of structure, from simple note-taking through to detailed behavioural checklists that are filled out at specific time intervals. So if we were interested in a specific work activity, we might begin our study by watching the activity take place and making some simple notes. Later, as we build up an understanding of the activity, we may develop more detailed checklists for recording specific activities.

Experimental method

This is possibly the most efficient method available to the behavioural scientist. Let us take the example of investigating the effect of alcohol on driving ability. One independent variable (alcohol) is manipulated, while all other potential influences are kept constant. The dependent variable (driving ability) is observed and recorded. If this behaviour changes significantly, the change may be logically attributed to the one variable (the independent, e.g. amount of alcohol consumed) that was deliberately varied.

Although the experimental method is an efficient and popular one, there are considerable problems to overcome.

(a) Extraneous variables are hard to control, as it is impossible to control the entire environment.

(b) Subjects may behave atypically (not in their usual way) because they are being studied).

(c) Laboratory-type setting is artificial and unnatural.

(d) Experimental study may often be unrealistically simple in an effort to aid research.

(e) Ethical issues arise in many experiments and should be considered. For example in the study of the effect of alcohol on driving ability, the researcher should take care that no harm could come to those involved in the study.

Observation and measurement are important concepts in behavioural science methods. Observation is important because it provides systematic recording of behaviour that falls into pre-selected behavioural categories. Measurement is important because it allows us to transform observations into a numerical scale. Behavioural science uses observation and measurement to translate psychological concepts into observable behaviours, then into data, which in turn can be subjected to analysis.

Behavioural science methodologies

Inquiry
Observation
Experimental

1.4.3 Validity

Any experimental research must fulfil the assumption of validity, that the research is actually studying what it says it is. There are two basic types of validity:

(a) **Internal validity** refers to the interpretation of internal relationships. An investigation has internal validity to the extent that changes in the independent variable (the variable thought to influence, determine or cause change in other variables) can be considered responsible for changes in the dependent variable (the specific behaviour observed or measured). For example, what effect does intelligence (independent variable) have on academic success (dependent variable)? In a study like that there would probably be high internal validity.

(b) **External validity** refers to the extent to which the findings of one particular study can be generalised to other populations and settings. Taking the example above, can the finding about the relationship of intelligence to academic success among a sample of schoolchildren be generalised to the entire Irish school population?

Behavioural science researchers recognise the difficulty in attaining a balance between internal and external validity, as findings from a (hopefully) representative sample are not always true for the entire population.

1.4.4 Scales of measurement

It is important for behavioural scientists to select the appropriate scale of measurement for a research design, one that accurately reflects the type of data collected. The scale employed determines the mathematical and statistical operations performed on the data. Generally, scientific disciplines distinguish four levels or scales of measurement: nominal, ordinal, interval and ratio.

(a) **Nominal** represents the lowest level of measurement, where observations are sorted into categories representing differences or similarities in kind. This scale makes only qualitative distinctions, such as male/female. There is no indication of differences in magnitude or quantity. Using this scale limits statistical treatments of data.

(b) **Ordinal** measurement permits an ordering of observations according to magnitude; this is a quantitative scale allowing assignment of numbers to observations to represent different amounts of a characteristic. Ordinal scales provide information on 'more' or 'less'; for example Grade A is higher than Grade B, which is higher than Grade C. There is, however, no indication of the amount of distance between grades. Grade A is not necessarily twice as good as B, nor B twice as good as C. This scale provides information on the relative positions of observations on a measured dimension, but no information on the distance between observations.

In relation to the final two levels of measurement we quote from Hair *et al.* (1992):

Interval and ratio scales provide the highest level of measurement precision. Thus they permit nearly all mathematical operations to be performed. These two scales have constant units of measurement, so differences between two adjacent points on any part of the scales are equal. The only real difference between interval and ratio scales is that interval scales have an arbitrary zero point, while ratio scales have an absolute zero point.

The most familiar **interval** scales are the Fahrenheit and Celsius temperature scales. Both have a different arbitrary zero point, and neither indicates a zero amount or lack of temperature, since we can register temperatures below the zero point of each scale. Therefore, it is not possible to say that any value on an interval scale is some multiple of some other point on the scale.

For example, an 80°F day cannot correctly be said to be twice as hot as a 40°F day because we know that 80°F, using a different scale, such as Celsius, is 26.7°C. Similarly, 40°F using Celsius, is 4.4°C. Although 80°F is indeed twice 40°F, one cannot state that the heat of 80°F is twice the heat of 40°F because, using different scales, the heat is not twice as great, that is 4.4°C x 2 ≠ 26.7°C.

Ratio scales represent the highest form of measurement precision, since they possess the advantages of all lower scales plus an absolute zero point. All mathematical operations are allowable with ratio scale measurements. The bathroom scale or other common weighing machines are examples of these scales, as they have an absolute zero point and can be spoken of in terms of multiples when relating one point on the scale to another; for example, 40 kilos is twice as heavy as 20 kilos.

1.4.5 Problems of behavioural science, in claiming to be a science

If behavioural scientists want to study behaviour scientifically, they must apply the goals of science. Immediately, problems spring to mind: how is it possible to measure aspects of the human character? Perhaps one of the most important issues: is it possible to remain objective when interpretation itself is a subjective process?

Human behaviour is rarely straightforward. Unlike natural science variables, people are constantly changing. The very topic of study or interest is often not observable. For example, how is it possible to study people's perceptions of a particular event when perception itself is a hypothetical construct, an unseen process.

The following table highlights behavioural science problems attached to each scientific goal.

GOAL	PROBLEM
DESCRIPTION (observation and measurement)	(a) **Deals with intangibles** (such as attitudes, motivation, perceptual processes).
	(b) **Multiplicity of variables**: People usually behave in a particular way for a combination of reasons.
	(c) **Precision is often elusive:** There may be a great deal of error due to the test or tester used.
	(d) **Behaviour may be unquantifiable** (how to measure motivation in people).
	(e) **Objectivity is difficult**, especially when dealing with behaviours we find personally distasteful such as racism.
UNDERSTANDING (cause and effect)	(a) **Often non-observable**: Perception and motivation are both internal and unseen processes.
	(b) **Unpredictability of human behaviour**: There is no guarantee human beings will act consistently in a given situation.
	(c) **Unreliability of relationships**: While we may establish a link between two experimental behaviours, often results are not replicated.
PREDICTION (outcomes)	(a) **Susceptible to research bias:** It can be tempting for researchers to influence outcomes in order to 'prove' their hypothesis.

GOAL	PROBLEM
PREDICTION (outcomes)	(b) **Internal variables susceptible to change:** Due to the effect of different mood states and emotions, participants' responses are not always predictable.
	(c) **Complexity and uniqueness of the individual:** No two people are alike, each will respond in her/his own unique fashion.
CONTROL	(a) **Ethical and moral constraints:** Behavioural scientists are bound by professional guidelines not to inflict mental or physical pain on human beings. This affects the range of work that can be carried out on human beings, especially as these guidelines prohibit potentially harmful deception on the part of the experimenter.
	(b) **Unforeseen extraneous variables:** The experimenters may have designed their experiment in the belief that certain conditions would apply. If these conditions change because of the effect of unforeseen or extraneous variables, the accuracy of results will be affected.
	(c) **Attempted manipulation of individuals by researcher:** Though it does not occur often, an experimenter may decide to choose individuals, or may influence people unduly so that a particular result is achieved.

This chapter has provided a general introduction to the discipline of behavioural science. Following a scientific path of inquiry gives it a platform for establishing a credible explanation of cause and effect—or the 'why' of human behaviour.

1.5 SUMMARY

1. Behavioural science is a collective concept encompassing disciplines such as psychology, sociology, anthropology and economics.

2. It is a science that attempts to remove personal bias and preconceptions from the interpretation of human behaviour by using the scientific method of inquiry.

3. It attempts to attain the goals of science, description, understanding, prediction and control.

4. It uses three basic research designs: inquiry, observation and the experimental method.

5. Four scales of measure are employed to aid statistical interpretation of data: nominal, ordinal, interval and ratio.

1.6 EXAM QUESTIONS

1. Outline a research design aimed at investigating consumers' preference for Brand X or Brand Y soft drink.

2. Describe the goals of science and any potential barriers to attaining such goals.

3. How might managers apply a knowledge of behavioural science?

4. Explain the concept of validity within research design.

5. In what circumstances would you use (a) a nominal scale and (b) an interval scale of measurement?

Chapter 2

Perception

Oh would some power the gift give us
To see ourselves as others see us!
It would from many a blunder free us.

Robert Burns (1759-1796)

2

Perception

Learning objectives

After studying this chapter, you should be able to:

1. *Define the processes of perception and sensation.*

2. *Describe the perceptual selectivity process with its accompanying perceptual cues.*

3. *Discuss perceptual organisation, with particular reference to Gestalt laws.*

4. *Understand an individual's perceptual world along with its influencing factors.*

5. *Identify the relevant variables that influence social perception.*

2.1 INTRODUCTION

Often viewed as a single process, perception actually consists of several distinct processes. Perception is interpretation (Logothetis, 1999). We do not have access to an objective reality, we only have an interpretative reality. Our reality is as we perceive it to be.

Perception is frequently defined as the process by which an individual selects, organises and interprets sensory stimuli into a meaningful picture of the world. In other words, perception is the way we 'see' the world around us. The many different phenomena we experience as humans means we are all remarkably different and complex individuals. It is logical that we should each have differing perceptions; what one person perceives as meaningful, another may perceive as false.

The perceptual process is common to us all; we use it to make sense of our environment. We must understand what is going on in order to assess and select the appropriate behavioural response required in a particular situation. A person's perception of a situation is not necessarily accurate, but it is that person's portrayal of the event.

This unique portrait is influenced by many variables or factors. For example, past experiences, motivations and expectations all have an effect on the perceiver. As noted by Kretch *et al.* (1962), an individual's perception of a given situation 'is not then a photographic representation of the physical world; it is, rather, a partial, personal construction'. Knowledge of the perceptual process is fundamental to understanding human behaviour. If we can understand how individuals view their world, we can begin to understand why they behave as they do.

This chapter has five main sections. Firstly, we discuss the concept of sensation and how it leads into the perceptual process. Secondly, we examine perceptual selectivity, how individuals select and at times dismiss environmental cues. Thirdly, we look at the process of perceptual organisation, how selected cues are organised in such a way as to aid understanding and interpretation. Fourthly, we investigate an individual's perceptual world and the processes that contribute to their own picture of the world. Lastly, we describe social perception, the process by which individuals make judgements and form opinions of others.

In marketing, it is important to realise that consumers act or react on the basis of their perceptions, not on the basis of objective reality. Products or services often have a symbolic value for consumers; reflecting their perceived self-image and the perceived product image. Consumers will often buy a product in the belief that it will enhance their perceived self-image (for example buying a perfume endorsed by a celebrity) or believe that by buying a perceived 'status' product, the status is in some way transferred to them. Knowledge of perceptual intricacies can aid marketers in determining what influences buying behaviour.

From an organisational viewpoint, a knowledge of perception helps management-employee relationships in a number of ways. For example, it ensures there is a shared interpretation of organisational goals; it helps to avoid inappropriate stereotyping, judgements and opinions during selection and appraisal procedures, and it enhances awareness of management and employee perceptual defence mechanisms.

Even in everyday situations, a knowledge of perception helps us to understand and cope with life. If we are aware of the process, we can be aware of how different cues trigger our attention and affect behaviour. We can begin to understand what causes us and others to see a situation in a particular way, and how people in general are very quick to form judgements and attribute causes to behaviours.

2.2 SENSATION

2.2.1 What is sensation?

We cannot have perception without first experiencing sensation. Sensation may be defined as the immediate and direct response of the sensory organs to simple stimuli.

A stimulus is anything that rouses a person to activity or produces a reaction in an organ or tissue of the body. The human body is equipped with five receptors through which it receives sensory data.

Receptor	Data
eyes	visual
ears	auditory
mouth	oral
skin	tactile
nose	smell

Information received through these receptors results in a corresponding sensation.

Sensation and perception co-exist. We need to be aware of stimuli before we can interpret them. Everyday we are bombarded with vast amounts of internal and external information: hunger or thirst (internal stimuli), sights and sounds of the world around us (external stimuli). Our sensory apparatus helps us to convert this array of information into various sensations. The detection and subsequent interpretation of this information is the distinction between sensation and perception.

There are two main differences between sensation and perception:

(a) **Duration:** Sensation is finite, meaning it has a limit or end. A smell will dissipate, a taste will fade. Perception on the other hand, is infinite, meaning there is no limit to our perceptual process. We are constantly perceiving and assessing situations and events.

(b) **Response:** Sensation is an immediate response to stimuli. Our nose responds directly and immediately to an odour without our consciously instructing it to do so. Perception will however always interpret stimuli. For example, our brain interprets the odour as pleasant or unpleasant and we respond accordingly. Perception can also block out our awareness of certain stimuli.

As sensation is finite, sensory data received must have a beginning and an end: a threshold.

2.2.2 Thresholds

Our sensory receptors possess limitations. The term commonly used is 'threshold', referring to the boundary between what the senses can and cannot pick up. For example, dog whistles are above the human auditory threshold. A number of sensory thresholds exist but we are primarily interested in two: the absolute threshold and the differential threshold.

Absolute threshold

This refers to the minimum stimulation necessary to be picked up by the human sensory receptors: the tickle of hair falling on your cheek or the pinprick of starlight just visible in a night sky. In other words, the absolute threshold refers to the lowest level at which an individual can experience a sensation.

Manufacturers use this principle when testing the general public for recognition of their product. Specifically, if they have spent a large budget on advertising a new product they want to test if the general public knows about it or retains any of its key attributes. If the market research shows they don't know about the product nor its attributes, that product will not have crossed the consumer's absolute threshold.

Differential threshold

This threshold is also referred to as either Weber's Law or the just noticeable difference (JND), and refers to the minimal difference that can be detected between two stimuli. It is important to note that the JND is not always an absolute or steady amount, but is relative to the intensity of the original stimulus.

In other words, if an individual picks up a 450 g bag of sugar in his right hand and then picks up a 450 g bag of sugar in his other hand, he tends to compare the weight between the two. The conclusion: the weights are similar. If, at this point, 50 g of sugar were added to the right hand making a total of 500 g, the individual would probably still perceive a similarity in the two weights. If, however, another 50 g were added to the right hand making a total of 550 g, the individual would just notice a difference between the two hands. A comparison of the left-hand weight with the right-hand weight (original stimulus) discerns a just noticeable difference between the two.

This JND occurs also in marketing and sales. The JND for customer awareness of sale prices is usually 20 per cent, all things being equal. In other words, 20 per cent discount tends to be the just noticeable difference between the original price (original stimulus) and the sale price, and is sufficient for people to act upon. This is not to say, however, that companies or stores could not spend large sums of money bringing a 5 per cent price reduction to consumers' notice. The JND is often explained as an increase or decrease in a stimulus that can be reliably detected as a change in amount, value or intensity.

The existence of a just noticeable difference can be seen when companies claim that there is a discernible difference between their products and others. This is particularly noticeable in relation to soft drinks and alcohol-based goods, which rely on taste to establish a difference between them and their competitors.

Producers of these products will claim that the taste difference between the products is more than just noticeable. To do this they will often make a 'taste test' part of their advertising campaign. They ask consumers to see if they can discern a difference between the unidentified products presented—one of which will include the product being advertised. Inevitably—for the purposes of the advertisement—the consumer will be able to perceive a difference between the products, usually in favour of the producer's brand. The product's producer then suggests that this perceived difference will add measurably to the consumer's enjoyment of the product.

Manufacturers of washing powders and household detergents also use this advertising technique when they show use visual examples of the performance of their products. An interesting 'twist' on this in recent years is the use of identical twins in television advertising to show the effect of personal care products such as skin and hair care treatments. The advert usually shows the twins side by side to emphasise the just noticeable difference if one uses the advertiser's product while the other uses a competitor's brand.

2.2.3 Habituation

This term is used when we stop paying attention to or noticing stimuli as they become familiar (Best, 1986). Our sensory apparatus no longer detects or attends to familiar stimuli. The ticking of a clock in a room is quite often not 'heard' because auditory receptors are acclimatised or habituated to the sound. If the ticking stops, we may 'miss' the noise and begin to focus on the silence. In the same way, parents are often habituated to their children's cries, but their visitors tend not to be. Many other examples spring to mind: the continuous shrill of a house alarm, 'sale' signs appearing in a shop window for months on end.

Manufacturers are particularly aware of the existence of habituation, as they realise that their customers may become 'tired' or 'bored' with a product. This is a type of habituation that may lead consumers to switch to another brand.

To encourage customer loyalty, producers often tell consumers that they have added benefits to their products, and emphasise this by changing the structure of their advertising campaign, as well as altering the product packaging and presentation. Popular fast-food outlets also issue new products to supplement their traditional range, often at discounted prices, so that their customers do not become bored with (or habituated to) the product range.

In summary, while habituation has obvious negative connotations, it does serve a purpose in simultaneously letting our sensory receptors 'deal' with familiar stimuli and yet allowing for fresh and novel aspects of our environment.

Although we can detect a multitude of stimuli, it is not physically possible to attend to them all. We therefore have to go on what is known as a selection process: selecting only stimuli that are relevant and meaningful to us. This is referred to as perceptual selectivity.

2.3 PERCEPTUAL SELECTIVITY

2.3.1 The selection process

We are constantly bombarded with environmental stimuli. If we had no way of protecting ourselves, it would be impossible to function effectively. We would become confused, mentally disorientated and unable to decide on how, or when, to act. Perceptual selectivity comes to our rescue. This is a process by which individuals actively select relevant stimuli from their surroundings.

A busy street full of stimuli.

Crossing a busy road requires perceptual selectivity. The list of stimuli vying for our attention, indeed bombarding our senses, is long: other pedestrians, traffic lights, vehicles, advertising signs, noise levels, shops, passers-by, a mass of information about our environment. As our intended behaviour is to cross the road, we must, and do, select only the stimuli that will help us initiate and achieve our goal. These may be vehicles, traffic lights and pedestrians. We have perceptually selected relevant stimuli from the environment, screening out the ones we do not need.

Perceptual selectivity occurs in many everyday situations. When using the phone, we focus on the voice at the other end and screen out distractions. At a party or a crowded bar, we screen out other people and focus on our partner's conversation. In marketing, perceptual selectivity enables the consumer to focus on, say, a newly advertised product and exclude the competing ones. For example, a fresh advertising campaign will gear itself to help the consumer to select perceptually its product by highlighting various features.

Selectivity may therefore be defined as a process through which we actively select stimuli, filtering or screening out information we do not need in order to prevent complete bombardment of the senses. It is a process influenced by factors in the object being perceived (external) and factors in the person who is perceiving (internal). These factors, known as **cues**, may be divided into two interdependent categories and referred to as external and internal cues.

2.3.2 External cues

External cues affect perceptual selectivity because of their physical properties. The observed characteristics of the stimulus activate or trigger our senses, thus heightening our awareness of its existence. External cues consist of:

(a) **Size:** The larger the stimulus the more likely it is to capture the perceiver's attention. However, a small object may be used as a contrast against large objects. Whether large or small, size represents an important variable.

In the case of mobile phones, the smaller the phone the more noticeable it is. The opposite is the case for petrol companies when they put large inflatable animals like tigers and gorillas on top of filling stations to catch people's attention.

(b) **Intensity:** The brighter the lights or the louder the sounds, the more they catch the attention. Television adverts are always louder in volume than programmes, so that viewers' attention will not wander during the commercial breaks. This can be seen with the very intense colour of the yellow reflective jackets worn by the police, and the bright red colours used for road signs indicating danger, for example STOP signs.

(c) **Contrast:** Objects that contrast strongly with their backgrounds are more likely to be perceived than less contrasting objects. Safety regulations tend to be headed by the word 'DANGER' in capital letters and in a contrasting colour to the rest of the message. Intense colours are used to contrast with other colours, as in the case of red brake lights on cars.

(d) **Novelty:** This refers to a stimulus that appears unique or unexpected, often seen in a familiar setting. It is based on the premise that confounding the perceiver's expectations of normality will make him/her focus on anything that is unusual or 'not normal'. Advertising campaigns put this principle to good use with talking vegetables and dancing animals. Humour (which we will examine briefly in the chapter on attitudes) is a very powerful type of novelty, though it does not last very long tending to wear off after two or three exposures.

(e) **Repetition:** The greater the number of times a message, word or name is repeated, the more attention is likely to be paid to it. (There is however a danger of habituation, which we looked at in section 2.2.3 above.) Advertising uses this principle when brand names, slogans and telephone numbers are repeated at the beginning and end of adverts. Repetition is almost a reinforcement mechanism, as we will see in the next chapter on learning and memory.

(f) **Movement:** We automatically focus on objects that move or give the impression of movement. Almost involuntarily our visual receptors, the eyes, follow any type of movement. We become aware of the moving object against its surroundings, e.g. neon lights flashing, rotary display cabinets and moving window displays. At Christmas, toy stores are famous for their mobile window displays which include the movement of puppets and toys.

In the same way, advertisers have maximised their income from billboard advertising by developing billboards that 'move'—the screen rotates to show a new product every few minutes—and which can almost simultaneously market three different products. Web-site developers are also keen to include movement in their sites, so that this will catch the eye of Internet users who log onto them. They do this by having figures that move, and by requiring the user to click on moving dialogue boxes.

External cues serve the purpose of heightening our awareness of stimuli by setting them apart from their surroundings. This works well, but is often not enough to hold our attention for more than a few moments. The effective use of external cues is essential for manufacturers in capturing the attention of consumers, particularly with brands that seem to have the same product benefits. For this reason, manufacturers will spend a great deal of their marketing budget on innovative packaging.

Companies that want to attract new employees also commission job advertisements that follow the same principles. This accounts for the increase in large, colour advertisements in the employment sections of many newspapers and magazines.

A second set of cues re-emphasises our awareness process; these are the internal cues.

2.3.3 Internal cues

Internal cues refer to the perceiver's personal factors, or internal variables, that are capable of influencing how much attention an individual pays to a particular stimulus. These feelings and experiences affect the way in which a person observes.

These internal variables or cues include:

(a) **Past experiences:** These play a large role in our perception of the present situation. If an individual has suffered an unpleasant experience, perhaps being bitten by a dog when a child, that individual may afterwards perceive dogs to be harmful creatures. It is the individual's experience, and therefore perception, that dogs are hurtful and not to be trusted. This is a very simplistic example, but it demonstrates why people react differently, and sometimes surprisingly, to the same stimuli.

(b) **Response salience:** This refers to the tendency to focus on objects that relate to our immediate wants or match our interests. If we are particularly interested in environmental matters, we pick up information about recycling. In other words, we are remarkably sensitive to information (stimulus) about something that is important to us.

   Take a photograph in a magazine. It could be a young girl sitting at a computer in her home. Two perceivers will focus on different stimuli within that photograph. An individual interested in the Internet focusses on the type of web site being accessed, while the second perceiver, an avid home decorator, concentrates on the surroundings of the child, particularly the colours or setting. What we need and what excites our interest are generally the things that guide our sensory receptors.

(c) **Response disposition**: This refers to a tendency to recognise familiar objects more quickly than unfamiliar ones. When advertising, companies keep the colours of products or the positioning of logos the same in an effort to aid the familiarisation process. A good example of this principle is Amnesty International, the human rights charity, with its distinctive logo of a candle wrapped in barbed wire.

(d) **Learning**: We have a learned predisposition to respond to certain stimuli, such as the colours that appear on certain consumer packaging. For instance, different cultures have learned for themselves that certain colours denote certain things. If we were to look at the packaging for the same product in different countries, it might be quite different. Marketers have to be aware of this when branding and packaging their product for a new market.

(e) **Intelligence**: How clever we are will affect what we pay attention to in the environment. Intelligent people often seek out a wide variety of stimuli, so as to stimulate their thought processes and so that they can develop new theories. Advertising copy aimed at them may be complex and may draw on various media.

(f) **Ability**: We tend to select elements from our environment which closely match the abilities we possess. If we have musical or artistic abilities, we are drawn to stimuli that incorporate these things. Artists or photographers are drawn to stimuli that are visually stimulating, while musicians sample from a wide variety of auditory sources. People often select the advertisements featuring abilities that they possess.

(g) **Training and education**: The more training and education someone receives in an area, the more they are able to attend to information which is presented to them. An engineer may be able to absorb large amounts of technical, mathematical data related to a car, for example, because of her/his academic training and education.

(h) **Interests**: We select out of the environment the aspects that most closely match what we are interested in. If you are interested in cycling, you would choose to see television programmes about mountain biking and the Tour de France. An interest in mountaineering would probably lead you to watch a programme on Mount Everest.

(i) **Goals and expectations**: Each person has expectations about their future. These are encapsulated in the goals that they set themselves. (See also Chapter 4 on motivation for more information.) Therefore they will choose information from the environment that is relevant to the goals they have set themselves. Someone wishing to follow a modelling career might select television programmes about 'supermodels' and may pay more attention to advertisements for cosmetics and fragrances.

(j) **Motivation**: Advertisers frequently appeal to motives when trying to attract attention to their products. Many women may tend to notice advertisements for beauty care products; parents may notice advertising involving children or parenthood, and many men often notice adverts involving high performance cars.

(k) **Personality**: Our personality may affect the way in which we select, or prefer, certain products. If we are outgoing and sociable, we might prefer to consume products with people like us, for example drinking alcohol in a busy, public place. If we are quiet and prefer intimate social settings, we may choose to focus on products that are consumed in this way—for example, renting or buying videos to watch at home.

(l) **Emotional state**: When you are angry or annoyed, you are less likely to be able to pay attention to what someone is saying. Conversely, when you are happy or in love, your perception of the world around you may be heightened, and you may select more stimuli.

(m) **Needs**: The needs of individuals affect their perception and what they choose as useful and relevant. Never go shopping when you are unhappy, as your need for affection may lead to you engaging in 'comfort buying'. The need for reassurance and affection is, in this case, substituted by purchasing and owning goods.

So, we can see that there are many internal cues that are important in perceptual selectivity. Although perceptual selectivity helps us select relevant stimuli, we still need to organise them in a way that makes sense. Reading these words is, in itself, a perceptual organisational task. Perceptual selectivity has enabled us to focus on the printed matter (using size/contrast cues), but it is perceptual organisation (the topic of the following section) that arranges the letters into words for us to interpret meaning.

2.4 PERCEPTUAL ORGANISATION

2.4.1 Organisation of stimuli

The name given to this patterning or organisation of stimuli is Gestalt, a German word literally translated as 'pattern'. Gestalt originates from a German school of psychology's study of perception. It believed that individuals did not view stimuli as separate components but organised them into a recognisable whole or pattern, and by so doing extracted meaning.

Take, for example, the printed word:

GESTALT

Perceptual selectivity enables us to select the lines, but it requires perceptual organisation—in the form of letters—to give the lines meaning. Gestalt takes this one step further by patterning the letters into one word—Gestalt—rather than leaving it as a string of separate letters. In the same way, if we refer to other people as good-looking, we are operationalising Gestalt. What we mean is that the person's eyes, skin, hair and mouth are all arranged in a way that is attractive, but rather than view the features as separate components, we organise them into a 'whole' view. The saying that 'the whole is greater than the sum of its parts' encapsulates the principle of Gestalt.

Gestalt may be defined as a process through which incoming stimuli are organised or patterned in a systematic and meaningful way. It is a dynamic process depending on interpretation to produce understanding.

2.4.2 Laws of Gestalt

The Gestalt or organising (sometimes referred to as patterning) of stimuli is not a unitary process. Gestalt encompasses three basic laws or rules, each with an individual core concept and contributing towards overall meaning and ease of interpretation.

These laws are:

(a)   Figure-Ground

(b)   Grouping

(c)   Closure

Law of figure-ground

While some aspects of a stimulus pattern appear to stand out as an object (figure), others provide a background (ground). This diagram illustrates this point.

Is this a vase or two faces looking at each other?

It is possible to interpret the stimulus as a vase (figure) against a black background (ground). Now alter your patterning of the stimuli, transforming the same picture into two dark profiles (figure) against a white background (ground). Similarly, the words on this page are figure, while the page is the ground. If you shift your patterning, the page becomes the figure and the writing the ground. Shifting from one perception to another allows an understanding of exactly what figure-ground organisation means.

The following figure is a well-known psychological portrait. Alter your perceptual patterning so you alternately see a young girl or an old woman.

Can you see a young girl or an old woman?

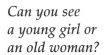

Law of grouping

We perceive stimuli in groups rather than singularly. We can pick out a letter in a word, but we tend to focus on the entire word. We group stimuli to enhance interpretation and meaning. This grouping rule encompasses three sub-laws.

(a) **Proximity**: Stimuli that are close together tend to be grouped together. The word 'deposed' appears in the following sentence:

FINDING WHO STOLE THE GARDEN SPADE POSED A PROBLEM

Because we group words together for ease of interpretation, we have to take time in trying to find the word. Once we have succeeded, it is possible to locate the word quickly a second time.

(b) **Similarity**: Stimuli that are similar in size, shape, colour, and form tend to be grouped together:

O O X O O

O O X O O

O O X O O

X X X X X X X X

O O X O O

O O X O O

O O X O O

What we see are a selection of crosses and circles, yet on the basis of similarity we tend to focus on the crosses or the four groups of six circles.

(c) **Logic**: Stimuli are grouped according to what the mind perceives as logically organised. For example:

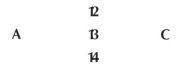

The interpretation of the middle figure depends on whether interpretation done is horizontally or vertically. Looking horizontally, the figure in the middle is B; looking vertically it is 13. We impose logic on our perceptual process to facilitate understanding.

Law of closure

The mind has a tendency to complete a figure or shape in order to achieve overall consistent form. Consider the following:

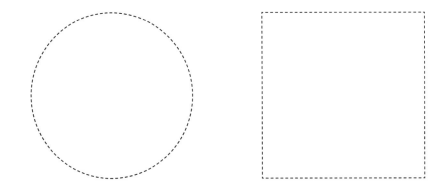

If asked to report what we see, we generally say a circle or a square. What we actually see are a collection of dashes approximating a particular shape. In the same way, the following is an example of how we can read sentences even when we are not presented with all of the information, as we can close or fill in the missing parts:

IT ISN T VE Y H R   TO   EAD HIS EN ENCE

We also have the ability to perform auditory closure tasks. If we hear snippets of conversation, we can usually fill in the gaps in order to understand the discussion. We need only hear snatches of a television signature tune to complete the rest of the tune or mentally 'close up' the programme. The signature tune will bring to mind the programme; we have closed up the tune and programme for ease of recognition. This is a commonly used technique in quiz shows.

Gestalt laws are the mind's attempt to place meaning and order on to stimuli. As humans, we always try to make meaning out of what we perceive. More often than not, individuals tend to be unaware of the effect that Gestalt principles have on their perceptual processes.

For example, we know the law of auditory closure eases our interpretation of a half-heard conversation, yet most individuals do this subconsciously, unaware that a perceptual process is taking place. Most people do not realise that Gestalt laws are partly responsible for different interpretations of the same stimuli. How we use these laws again depends on the individual.

2.5 THE INDIVIDUAL'S PERCEPTUAL WORLD

2.5.1 Unique views

In section 2.3 we discussed the selectivity of perception and why people notice some things and ignore others. Here we examine how two people who notice the same thing can put different meanings on what they see. Two people can watch the same film but 'see' different things. Why is this so?

2.5.2 Categorisation

Our perceptual learning builds up a set of personal mental categories to which our experiences are assigned and labelled. These perceptual categories are tremendously influential. Researchers Langer and Abelson (1974) showed a 15-minute video interview to a class of psychotherapists. Half were told the interviewee was applying for a job as a trainee psychotherapist, the other half that the interviewee was a mental patient. Those who had categorised the interviewee as an applicant, perceived him as being realistic, sincere and pleasant. Those who categorised him as a mental patient, perceived him as defensive and impulsive. In each case the trainee psychotherapists used their mental categorisation systems to label the interviewee according to categorisation criteria.

This example indicates clearly how powerful and influential our categorisations are. Frequently we are unaware that our categorisation system is operating and we behave according to how we unconsciously interpret the situation.

2.5.3 Perceptual expectancies

Past experience, motives, context and suggestion all help to create a perceptual expectancy. We are set to perceive in a certain way and respond by seeing what we expect to see. Many perceptual expectancies are created by suggestion, as is demonstrated by the following two pieces of research.

(a) A psychology professor arranged an experiment in which a guest lecturer taught two of his classes. Beforehand one class was told the lecturer was a 'rather cold person'; the other that he was a 'rather warm person'.

After the lecture, each group of students was interviewed. Students who received the 'cold' description perceived the lecturer as unhappy, irritable and did not participate in class. Those who received the 'warm' description saw the lecturer as happy and good-natured and did participate.

(b) A group of psychology students of the University of Oregon were asked to assess the facial expression of a picture of a man in his late fifties chosen at random by the researchers. Half were told he was in the Gestapo during the Second World War and responsible for horrific medical experiments on concentration camp inmates. Not surprisingly, the group judged his expression to be cruel and frowning. The students who were told he was a life-saving Resistance hero judged his expression as warm and friendly (Rothbart and Birrell 1977).

The implications of perceptual expectancies on the perceptual process are immense.

2.5.4 Selective perception

This process enables us to screen out information we do not wish to see or hear. It is similar to the general perceptual selectivity process but involves to a greater degree the internal aspects of the personality. For instance, psychologically we often want only to hear or believe information that reaffirms our picture of the world. We do not want to focus on information that may be at odds with our beliefs or values.

Consumers buying product 'seconds' will often screen out the damage or poor quality of the product to maintain the bargain's positive aspects. Individuals often select only those traits they wish to see in friends or acquaintances, ignoring the more negative aspects. The old cliché 'love is blind' in fact describes selective perception.

2.5.5 Perceptual defences

This process enables us to protect ourselves psychologically from threatening stimuli. In other words, rather than face up to an unpleasant or menacing situation, we either select an alternative, or distort or ignore threatening stimuli.

We operate our perceptual defence mechanisms when we feel we cannot cope with the reality of our present situation or when our long-held beliefs are challenged, as when for example cigarette smokers often gloss over the government health warning printed on cigarette packets.

It is important to note that perceptual defences may increase the difficulty of a situation because of the non-acceptance or distortion effected by the individual. Perceptual defence exists for all people, whether they hold what we might believe are reasonable or unreasonable views of the world.

Perceptual defence is often used when we are presented with information in advertisements intended to 'warn' us against some practice that may harm us. In this sense, perceptual defence is an important issue for government health authorities presenting the public with health promotion advertisements, particularly in relation to smoking and healthy lifestyle choices. The smoker may feel that the message being presented—usually involving graphic accounts of the dangers of smoking—is too threatening to their current view of the world.

If this happens, the smoker may choose to ignore the information, or may defend themselves against its claims by distorting the reality of their own situation. They might, for example, rationalise the advertisement by saying it does not apply to them as they are a 'social' smoker, who only smokes when having a drink with their friends in a pub. They have therefore chosen to distort the health promotion message that it doesn't matter where or when you smoke, it is still bad for your health.

The challenge in this instance is to present a message which is not so threatening that the people it is aimed at immediately distort the information. To do this, advertisers must present information that is not overly upsetting or threatening to their viewers.

Some believe that the opposite should be the case. They think that it is only if you show the consequences of certain actions on others that the individual, and those who tacitly support him/her, will consider changing their actions. So while anti-smoking adverts present to individuals the consequences of their actions: shortened life expectancy and inevitable reliance on health-care services; anti-drink driving and anti-speeding adverts show how these actions do not exist in a vacuum and often have fatal consequences for innocent bystanders.

In these cases, the advertisers are trying to shock the individuals concerned so that they change their behaviour. This is done in the belief that drink-drivers and those who break the speed limit distort the messages from ordinary anti-drink driving and anti-speeding advertising, but may not be able to do so with an extreme message.

Unfortunately, there are some individuals who still are able to rationalise their behaviour and distort what is a plain and self-evident message. They are engaging in perceptual defence.

2.5.6 Attribution

The link between this process and perception is quite simple: people rarely perceive behaviour; they infer causes at the root of behaviour. People's interpretation of behaviour goes beyond the actual behaviour, they tend to interpret the cause or intention of the behaviour. If they can interpret the cause of behaviour, they feel they understand the situation better.

Kelley (1980) noted the existence of both internal and external attributions, or causes. People determine the causes of behaviour both in themselves and in others by:

(a) **Internal attribution:** Behaviour is due to a person's own skill, ability or talent, for example Joanne is successful because she works very hard.

(b) **External attribution:** Behaviour is due to chance, ease of situation or aid given, for example Frank passed his driving test because the driving instructor was extremely lenient.

Three factors come into play when we attempt to 'read' causes in the behaviour we perceive: **consensus, consistency** and **distinctiveness.** Take, for example, two children in a classroom situation, both exhibiting loud behaviour. The teacher perceives Claire in a far more negative light than Tom. Why?

The teacher's attribution process is at work. She is assigning causes to each child's behaviour—remember we do not perceive behaviour as much as behaviour which is caused. The teacher assigns an internal, almost deliberately negative cause, to Claire, that Claire is being rowdy because she enjoys being disruptive, while Tom is assigned an external cause, that Tom is being rowdy because the rest of the class is also being noisy. Claire is deliberately annoying; Tom is being influenced by others. How is this attribution arrived at? The teacher is using the three attribution factors.

(a) **Consensus**: The extent to which a group member is acting in accordance with the group.

(b) **Consistency**: The extent to which the observed person behaves in the same way in this, and other similar, situations.

(c) **Distinctiveness**: The extent to which the observed individual behaves idiosyncratically when faced with different situations.

If we go back to Claire and Tom:

Claire is rowdy, regardless of her companions' behaviour. She is always rowdy in this teacher's class. In fact, she is rowdy in every situation, whether in class, at home or in the playground.

Tom is rowdy because the whole class is rowdy. His behaviour tends to be influenced by the general class behaviour. He tends not to be disruptive in any other area of life, whether at play or at home.

Attribution theory has important implications within an organisational setting. Where management attributes poor performance levels to internal causes, for example Daniel is not performing well because he is not motivated, employee-management relationships may suffer. It may well be the case that Daniel is performing poorly merely because he does not experience adequate resource back up.

It is interesting to note that when we make attributions about ourselves we claim internal attributions for positive results, for example I won the lottery because I used my family's birthdays for numbers, and external attributions for negative outcomes, for example I didn't win because the numbers were all low and therefore unusual.

We have seen that an individual's perceptual world is far from simple. There are many interrelating variables influencing our view of our world. If the process of viewing the environment is fraught with difficulties, is the process of viewing other people also complex? We now examine what is involved when all the components of the perceptual process are targeting another individual, known as social perception.

2.6 SOCIAL PERCEPTION

2.6.1 Views of others

Social perception is an important part of the perceptual process. It is how we perceive, or 'see', other people. As we have learned, perception is an individual and complex process even when viewing events or situations not directly affecting us. Think how much more prone to errors our 'people' perception must be.

Inaccurate perception has important consequences. In the workplace, misperceptions of attitudes and motivations can have severe repercussions in the workforce. In marketing, consumer misconceptions of a marketing campaign may cause brand failure. In everyday life, misperceptions of other people may cause us to miss out on friendships or to 'label' people incorrectly.

How then do we perceive people? What cues do we focus on? What do we selectively screen out? What errors do we make? There are three basic interactive influences affecting our perceptions of others:

(a) Characteristics of the person perceived.

(b) Characteristics of the perceiver.

(c) Characteristics of the situation.

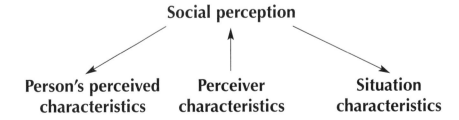

Social perception

Person's perceived characteristics   Perceiver characteristics   Situation characteristics

2.6.2 Characteristics of the person perceived

We tend to perceive and form impressions of other people on two levels: on one consciously taking in their unique set of personal characteristics, on the other unconsciously absorbing and interpreting according to our categorisation system. Specific influences on our interpretations include:

(a) **Physical appearance**: This includes age, gender, height, weight and dress.

(i) **Age**: Our perception of someone's age may have a bearing on how well we feel they can perform certain tasks. We might expect that a surgeon should have a great deal of experience, and so should be older, whereas we might expect that a popular musician should be younger as this is an area for younger people.

Recent employment legislation has sought to ban discrimination on the basis of age, as it was found that certain employers were making decisions not to recruit based on misconceptions of what people of certain ages could and could not do.

(ii) **Gender**: Our own gender, and the gender of those around us, strongly affects how we perceive other's gender. Based on someone's gender, we may see a person as a mother or father figure, a potential partner, or someone with whom we can form a friendship.

Gender relations may not always be clear cut, as there may be confusions as to what is the appropriate behaviour towards members of the opposite gender to us. We may have a belief in how that gender should conduct itself. The changes which took place in women's roles in the home and in the workforce in the twentieth century created a great deal of debate about male and female roles in society.

(iii) **Height**: The perception of a person's height is often linked with power relations. Tall people may be perceived as being commanding and in control and so may be chosen as leaders. History is full of examples of tall leaders, including General de Gaulle in France and Eamon De Valera in Ireland, but we can also see examples of smaller leaders such as Napoleon. This would suggest that the personality of the leader is more important in determining their popularity. Nevertheless, height has an effect on how we relate to those around us, as our height relative to others affects our perception of them, and vice versa.

(iv) **Weight**: In our society today, there is a great deal of emphasis on slimming and on leading a healthy lifestyle. For this reason, there are many photographs of the 'ideal' body and appearance, often a very thin model. Sociologists have suggested that this has affected what we perceive as 'normal' weight, even though very thin people only form a small percentage of our population. This may lead to people who are not this thin being perceived as being overweight or fat, which brings with it some preconceptions about self discipline about food.

It is perhaps best to remember that different people have different 'body forms', which affect how they look, irrespective of the quality and quantity of what they eat. In spite of this, individuals make assumptions about us based on our perceived weight.

(v) **Dress**: The concept of power dressing, begun in the United States, quickly spread worldwide. People wearing business suits suggest status and professionalism. We feel secure when we see doctors dressed in white coats, leading to a high number of television adverts with 'professionals' wearing white coats when promoting toothpaste, household bleach and dietary products. Uniforms in general signal efficiency, expertise and responsibility.

(b) **Verbal communication**: This covers accents, tones of voices, articulateness. **Accents** can give geographical, social and educational cues. Note how 'soap operas' depict characters from a specific social class. **Tone or pitch of voice** offers perceptions of personality types; high pitch can indicate nervousness, while a more even tone of voice gives an impression of confidence.

Articulateness: Choice and use of words also contribute to social perception. Those who are more articulate are often perceived— wrongly sometimes—as being more intelligent. The lack of articulateness in a social setting may be due to lack of self-confidence or even shyness, rather than levels of intelligence.

(c) **Non-verbal communication:** Body language is unconsciously transmitted through various channels, such as face, eyes or posture. We subconsciously pick up and respond to these signals, creating a sub-level of communication of which we may not be aware.

Avoiding eye contact is considered bad manners in some cultures, giving the impression that the person who does not make eye contact is not paying attention. Anthropology has shown us that in some cultures it is considered rude to maintain constant eye contact. When this culture encounters another one that believes in eye contact, there can be misunderstanding.

Continuous posture shifting may denote psychological unease and spatial considerations imply relationship difference, for example physical space between employee and boss is always much wider than the space between two friends.

(d) **Ascribed attributes:** We tend to perceive people according to their ascribed attributes, such as status, occupation. The higher the status, the more we may see the person as capable and self-assured. Similarly, professions seem to evoke more esteem than, say, administrative jobs. In each case, the person is being judged not for himself but for his ascribed attributes. Often we hear the complaint from media celebrities that people respond to them not as mortals but as stars, an ascribed attribute.

2.6.3 Characteristics of the perceiver

The characteristics or make-up of the perceiver (the person doing the looking) also play an important role in person perception. Many of these characteristics are similar to internal cues examined in section 2.3 above on perceptual selectivity and can greatly influence the way we look and feel towards another person. These include:

(a) **Self concept:** This refers to the picture we have of ourselves. If we accurately understand ourselves, we tend to accurately perceive other people. Research indicates the more accepting we are of ourselves, the more accepting we are of, and less threatened by, other people (Steers, 1991).

(b) **Cognitive structure:** Our ability to perceive others is based on multiple criteria. The more we can differentiate between people, using multiple variables and characteristics such as pleasant, hardworking and reliable, the more accurate our perception will be.

(c) **Previous experience with the individual**: Earlier experiences influences our perception. An unpleasant incident involving an individual in the past causes us to categorise or label that person negatively. We find it very difficult to alter our opinion of that person in the future, even when presented with evidence showing the person in a positive light. It is very hard to rid ourselves of this first impression.

2.6.4 Characteristics of the situation

Two situational influences affecting our social perception are: the location (where the initial meeting took place and under what conditions) and the company (the people with whom we are observed).

(a) **Location**: Whether the location or surroundings are formal or informal can alter a person's perception. Meeting someone for the first time in a formal situation like an interview can give a certain impression; meeting again later in a less formal setting like a party causes us a certain amount of confusion. It is extremely difficult to switch perceptions once we have 'tied' people to a particular setting. It is rather like not recognising a work colleague in a social setting.

(b) **Company**: The people we are observed with often have a part to play in another's perception of us. Individuals tend to group or label others for ease of identification. We often categorise a person by the company he or she keeps. This in itself is not a fault as long as we do not err in our judgements.

2.6.5 Influencing factors

Individual differences account for a tremendous amount of subjectivity and unreliability (including distortions) in perception. This is particularly true for our perception of a person, when the process of perception is influenced, or biased, by a number of factors:

- Halo effect.
- Stereotyping.
- Projection.
- Personality beliefs.
- First impressions.
- Attribution bias.

(a) **Halo effect**: A judgement or perception of a person is often made on the basis of one characteristic, such as politeness. We tend then to attribute to that person other similar and logical (to us) characteristics, such as honesty, cheerfulness and reliability. We do not know if these other characteristics exist within the person observed, but we believe so purely on the basis of the one observed characteristic.

For example, if we met someone who worked for a charity we might infer that they were a caring, generous person. They might just be someone who is a professional organiser who happened to work for a charity and who does not have these characteristics. We might also meet a successful businessperson and assume they are hard-working, visionary and entrepreneurial, whereas they might have none of these characteristics and might simply have worked within a large organisation which ensured their success. This has been termed the positive halo effect.

The opposite can also be the case, that we perceive a person negatively on the basis of a small, and possibly unrepresentative, set of characteristics. This is known as the negative, or rusty, halo effect. In this instance, we might meet someone with a 'cultured' accent, and presume that they are a snob who looks down on everyone else. Once again, we do not know if these characteristics exist within the person perceived, but we are presuming them from one characteristic, the accent. In the same way, we might find out that another person is a supporter of a political party we do not like and so we might believe that they want power and influence over people.

(b) **Stereotyping**: We have a tendency to judge people according to the group to which we feel or perceive they belong. We want to categorise or label people so we can 'place' them in our minds and attribute to them a set of expected characteristics. Instead of dealing with people on an individual level, we often stereotype them as representatives of a particular group or class.

In fact, this act of stereotyping can be useful. It reduces ambiguity, enables us to classify people quickly and simplifies our interpersonal world. However, it can also lead to misperception and loss of individuality on the part of the person perceived.

Stereotyping is done in many different ways, including negative attitudes to people:

Nationality	We frequently classify nations, for example Americans are loud, Germans are serious, Irish are happy-go-lucky.
Race/Ethnicity	We may believe that black people have a natural sense of rhythm or that an Arab is an extreme religious fundamentalist.
Age	Older workers are less able to change than a young workforce because they are opinionated and set in their ways.
Gender	Men make better leaders than women; women make better homemakers and child rearers than men.
Religion	Some believe that all Catholics suffer from guilt due to their sexuality or that all Jewish people are selfish with money.
Sexuality	A common stereotype of gay people is that homosexuals are effeminate and lesbians have aggressive male characteristics.

(c) **Projection:** This occurs when we attribute to others similar characteristics or feelings that we ourselves experience. We often make inferences about the causes of people's behaviour based purely on what we would do or feel in a similar situation. This can be inappropriate in an organisational setting when we attribute negative motives to the actions of others based on what we would do in a particular setting.

For example, a person may arrive late not due to poor timekeeping (the reason we may be late) but because they have a new child and have a long distance to travel. If we believed the cause of their lateness to be poor timekeeping, we would be projecting onto them what we do in the same situation.

(d) **Personality beliefs**: This refers to the 'implicit personality theory' we all possess. That is, we use limited information about a person for generalisation purposes. We believe certain personality traits 'go with' other personality traits—jolly and fat; hardworking and honest; talkative and extraverted. Because of this implicit personality theory, we tend largely to 'create' an image or perception of a person.

(e) **First impressions**: These tend to be long-lasting and difficult to contradict. First impressions trigger our perceptual set, so we see a person in a particular way that has already been decided upon. Webster (1982) indicates that unskilled interviewers make tentative first impressions or judgements about interviewees within the first four minutes of the interview, spending the remaining interview time selecting information that conforms with, and confirms, these first impressions.

(f) **Attribution bias**: As we know from section 2.5.6 above, attribution theory deals with allocating reasons for people's behaviour—either on an internal or external basis. Attribution is, however, vulnerable to the following errors:

  (i) **Intention**: An act, viewed as intending to gain a reward, tends to be seen in a less positive light (external attribution) than an act which is perceived as unselfish or having no ulterior motive (internal attribution). If, say, a celebrity advertises sports shoes and is disclosed as a director of the manufacturing company, the credibility of both celebrity and product is viewed differently by the consumer. The general consumer attribution may well be that the celebrity is 'only doing it for the money'.

  (ii) **Status**: The status of a person we perceive affects how we attribute causes to their behaviour. The higher the status, the more responsible for his/her actions the person is perceived to be.

  (iii) **Self-serving bias**: When anything positive happens to us, we tend to attribute internal causation (e.g. I set the wheels in motion), while to anything negative we attribute external causation (i.e. if the time had been right the business would have succeeded). Curiously, we tend to do the opposite when attributing causes of other people's behaviour. It is common practice for management to attribute an employee's non-performance or failure to the individual's own efforts (internal attribution) rather than to the actual work situation or the employee's supervisors (external attribution).

The above demonstrates the complexity of social perception. Far from making simple judgements about a person or their actions, we unconsciously engage in many processes that may or may not give accurate results. We must at all times be aware of such influences.

This chapter has examined the complexity of the human perceptual process and its ability to make sense of our environment. If we are to understand why people behave as they do, we must first understand how they view the world. Each person possesses his/her own perceptual world.

2.7 SUMMARY

1. Perception is a process whereby individuals select, organise and interpret stimuli in order to give meaning to their environment.

2. Sensory receptors receive incoming stimuli in the form of sensations but do not interpret them.

3. Perceptual selectivity is the process whereby individuals actively select and screen out stimuli to prevent bombardment of the senses. This is influenced by external and internal cues.

4. Perceptual organisation—GESTALT—enables us to organise stimuli into a meaningful picture of the world.

5. An individual's perceptual world consists of many variables including selective perception, perceptual defence, categorisation, expectancies, attributions.

6. Person perception involves three variables, perceived, perceiver, and situation, and is influenced by many factors such as halo effect, stereotyping, attribution bias and projection.

2.8 EXAM QUESTIONS

1. Discuss the ways in which sensation differs from perception.

2. Discuss how the physical properties of stimuli are important variables in gaining people's attention. (MII, 1998)

3. Describe the ways in which human beings organise incoming stimuli. Why is such organisation necessary? (MII, 1997)

4. Describe the 'errors' that may occur in how we perceive others. (MII, 1997)

5. Analyse the theories of the Gestalt school of psychology in relation to our perception of objects and of people. Suggest some ways in which it could be applied to the work of a manager. (Institute of Technology, Tallaght, 1999)

Chapter 3

Learning and Memory

As the child moves within the social world of
the classroom, she appropriates (internalises)
but also reconstructs the discourses that
constitute the social world of her classroom.
This creative process is what
I would term learning.

Deborah Hicks (1996)

3

Learning and Memory

Learning objectives

After studying this chapter, you should be able to:

1. *Understand what learning is.*

2. *Describe and explain the Behaviourist approach to learning.*

3. *Describe and explain the Cognitive school of learning.*

4. *Identify the differences between the Behaviourist and Cognitive approaches.*

5. *Be familiar with the stages of memory and understand some of the reasons why we forget.*

3.1 INTRODUCTION

It seems self-evident that as human beings we have the ability to learn many things: to walk and talk, to develop relationships and to learn new skills. Although it may appear that this 'just happens' and is a natural part of our humanity, it is in fact part of a learning process.

In later chapters we examine how individuals learn to live in society, to adopt approved behavioural roles and to harmonise within their culture. However, at present we are interested in how individuals learn responses, behaviours and skills. Many theories offer themselves as frameworks from which we can study learning behaviour and we will examine some in this chapter.

Why are we interested in learning? From an organisational point of view, we aim to promote employee adaptation to organisational goals. This includes areas such as training, performance levels, motivation and, most importantly, it establishes a clear work-reward learning relationship. From a marketing perspective, we hope to be able to shape consumers' buying behaviour. The more advertising agencies discover how a consumer learns, the better they are able to develop their campaigns. In everyday real life, we understand that learning or the ability to learn links us to our world. If we could not learn, we would be immediately set apart from our peers. We teach children basic tasks; we teach animals basic tricks; and we teach ourselves basic skills. Learning is an inherent part of being human.

Imagine you are a manager and you wish to implement a training programme to update your employees' technical skills. You want to promote the value of participating in the training programme, but how do you do this? Should you set goals for employees, offer rewards, threaten sanctions, or give feedback based on performance targets? There are many ways of understanding and approaching human learning. In the sections that follow we outline the schools of thought that underpin learning and training initiatives. We examine first the Behaviourist school of learning, i.e. the conditioning approach to learning, and secondly the Cognitive school, i.e. the information-processing approach. These two schools tend to be viewed as mutually exclusive, yet they have certain areas of agreement. We evaluate both models.

The final section in this chapter includes a model of memory. We look at how people remember, how they retrieve stored information and under what circumstances they forget. It would seem obvious to most people that learning must involve the memory system. We hope to present a clear and unambiguous model of memory that contributes to our task of understanding human behaviour.

In studying learning, we first offer a definition to ground the concept (Coon, 1986):

> Learning may be defined as a relatively permanent change in behaviour occuring as a result of experience or practice.

3.2 BEHAVIOURIST LEARNING THEORIES

The Behaviourist school has four major proponents, each contributing to the behaviourist model:

(a) Ivan Pavlov.   (c) E.L. Thorndike.

(b) John Watson.   (d) B.F. Skinner.

Each considered learning a process of conditioning, association and reinforcing. They believed in the concept of learning laws, applicable to all, regardless of environmental or social variables. We concentrate on two: Ivan Pavlov and classical conditioning, and B.F. Skinner's operant conditioning.

3.2.1 Classical conditioning

Russian physiologist Ivan Pavlov (1849-1936) believed in the concept of **association**. This, he felt, was the only way learning would occur. Pavlov's classical conditioning is built upon respondent behaviour: that is, reflexes that are directly elicited by certain stimuli.

Ivan Pavlov, Russian psychologist

As basis for conditioning, Pavlov used the reflexive salivary response of a dog to the smell of food. He believed he could link, or associate, the stimulus (food) that elicited the reflexive response (salivation) to another stimulus, which would in turn elicit the same response. To prove it, he attempted to link the smell of food with the sound of a bell, so that the dogs would salivate at the sound of the bell, without the food being presented. In other words, Pavlov hoped to 'teach' a dog to salivate at the sound of a bell.

In the experiment Pavlov used four variables:

(a) **Unconditioned stimulus:** Natural or unlearned stimulus.

(b) **Unconditioned response:** Natural or unlearned response.

(c) **Conditioned stimulus:** Stimulus that acquires the ability to elicit a response after being associated with an unconditioned stimulus.

(d) **Conditioned response:** Learned response that follows an unconditioned stimulus and conditioned stimulus pairing.

Pavlov observed that when he gave the dogs in his laboratory pieces of meat (unconditioned stimulus) they would salivate (unconditioned response), as is natural since salivation aids digestion. The meat was obviously the stimulus as it evoked the response of salivation within the dogs. Both were unconditioned in the sense that the dogs did not have to be trained to react in this way.

Pavlov set out to try and match the unconditioned response (UCR) to a conditioned stimulus (CS). In this case, Pavlov wanted to see if he could make the dogs salivate (conditioned response, as it would now be) when he presented them with the sound of a bell (conditioned stimulus) (Pavlov, 1927). The means by which he did this involved:

Stage 1:   Presenting the dogs with a piece of meat (unconditioned stimulus) and observing them salivate (unconditioned response).

Stage 2:   Presenting the dogs with a piece of meat (unconditioned stimulus) and ringing a bell at the same time (conditioned stimulus), and then observing them salivate. This was repeated until the dogs were familiar with the sound of the bell. Note that Pavlov was trying to **pair**, or associate, the sound of the bell with the meat in order for the bell sound to gain the power of the unconditioned stimulus.

Stage 3:   Ringing the bell (conditioned stimulus) and observing the dogs salivate (conditioned response).

Pavlov succeeded; he conditioned the dogs to associate the sound of the bell with the meat, and was able to bring about a salivation response. Pavlov's classical conditioning may be defined as when 'a previously neutral stimulus begins to elicit a response through **association** with a paired stimulus' (Pavlov, 1927). The dogs eventually associate the bell and food with one another; Pavlov succeeded in teaching them a behaviour through conditioning.

The same phenomenon occurs when for example someone in our family says, 'Tea's ready.' When we hear this phrase, though we may not have either smelt nor tasted the food, we will probably start salivating. In this case, the conditioned stimulus is the phrase 'tea's ready' and the conditioned response is salivation.

A number of Pavlovian concepts were drawn from the above:

(a)   **Stimulus generalisation:** This is the effect generated by one stimulus that can be transposed to another similar stimulus. For example, Pavlov discovered that if he sounded a buzzer, the dogs found it sufficiently like the bell that it evoked the same response, salivation. When we are in a friend's house and hear the doorbell, we are still conditioned to answer the door even though the doorbell may not sound exactly like our own. In this case, we are generalising the knowledge of the sound of our own doorbell to that of the house we are in.

(b) **Extinction:** This occurs when we remove an important part of the stimulus-response mechanism. Pavlov stated that if an important stimulus were removed for a sufficiently long period, the conditioned response would eventually disappear. During his experiments, he discovered that if he presented the bell for a number of trials without the meat, the salivation response disappeared, or became **extinct.** Thus, a conditioned response (salivation) will not last indefinitely unless reinforced by the unconditioned stimulus (meat). The same effect occurs when a manufacturer advertises a 'free' offer, which turns out to be nothing of the sort. After purchasing the product a few times without reward, the effect will become extinct and the consumer will stop believing the manufacturer's claims.

(c) **Spontaneous recovery:** Once the effect of the conditioned stimulus (the bell) has been extinguished, we can re-present the unconditioned stimulus (the meat in this case, along with the bell) and it will once again become effective. This process is known as spontaneous recovery. Pavlov discovered the dogs began to salivate when he re-presented the meat after an absence. This can also happen in the world of marketing when a producer reintroduces special offers, which had initially induced customers to buy the product.

(d) **Higher order conditioning:** This is the transposition of one conditioned stimulus to another. Pavlov discovered that if he presented a card showing a black dot at the same time as a bell sounded, the dogs would begin the association process and salivate at the sight of the card. He termed this **higher order conditioning.** It differs from stimulus generalisation because the bell and the buzzer are presented separately in stimulus generalisation, whereas the bell and card are presented together in higher order conditioning. Advertisers try to achieve a similar effect when they attempt to associate a number of desirable images with their product.

Both Pavlov and Skinner understood human learning in terms of stimulus-response (S-R) bonds, and it is to Skinner's model of learning that we now turn.

3.2.2 Operant conditioning

B.F. Skinner (1904-1990) is one of the most important psychologists of the twentieth century. He took Pavlov's work further and developed it to such an extent that his own findings have found uses in situations as disparate as acknowledging and enhancing employee performance in the workplace and shaping social behaviour in mental hospitals. There are few areas in which his theories have not been applied.

B.F. Skinner

Skinner attempts to offer an accurate description of the ways we learn and are capable of adjusting our behaviour in changing circumstances (Skinner, 1953). Basically, operant conditioning may be defined as when 'an individual operates on, or is instrumental in, the environment to produce a change that leads to a reward'.

The key factor for Skinner is reinforcement. A number of Skinnerian concepts were drawn from the above principles:

(a) **Positive and negative reinforcement**: Skinner introduced this notion, demonstrating it in terms of responses from rats in what became known as a **Skinner box**. For example, when a rat touched a lever in the box, it was rewarded by food. Skinner declared the behaviour had **been positively reinforced** (and thus learned), and that a simple stimulus (rat touching the lever) response (rat receives food) bond was in operation.

When we buy a product and receive a money-off voucher, we are being positively reinforced, and are more likely to repeat our actions to gain another voucher. Manufacturers have 'taught' us to buy their products. In contrast, **negative reinforcement** involves the removal of an unwanted stimulus; for example prisoners, in return for good behaviour, receiving 'time off' their sentences.

If, however, the rat had touched the lever and received a slight electric shock, Skinner would declare it had been been **punished** and unlikely to repeat the action. According to Skinner, the rat had **learned** not to press the lever. An everyday example of punishment is a driver receiving a fine for speeding. This punishment (fines) may continue until the driver realises that to avoid the fine it is necessary to drive within speed limits.

The importance of the notion of positive and negative reinforcement lies in the ability of the person (or animals) concerned to elicit a positive or negative response from those who supply the reinforcement. In other words, in Skinner's analysis of learning, his subjects were able to influence their environment through recognising and responding to reinforcement techniques. Pavlov's subjects were passive, while Skinner's played an active part in their behavioural consequences.

(b) **Selective reinforcement and discriminative stimulus:** Skinner also introduced the concepts of selective reinforcement and discriminative stimulus. For example, he tried selectively reinforcing his rats' behaviour by rewarding the pressing of the lever only when a light was shining. The rat learned to press the lever only when there was a continuous light; the light serving as the discriminative stimulus. 'Happy hours' in pubs operate on the same principle, rewarding customers for drinking during particular times by offering cheaper drinks.

(c) **Partial and continuous reinforcement:** Partial reinforcement is random rewarding of the subject. The other is continuous rewarding of the subject for his/her actions. For example, partial reinforcement would occur if the rat in Skinner's box was rewarded for five out of ten lever presses. Continuous reinforcement occurs if the rat was rewarded for each press. Skinner noted that behaviour partially reinforced lasted longer, as the rats tended to repeat their actions in the expectation of a reward.

Partial reinforcement is often used in marketing by rewarding consumers with bonus points (on a store card or a frequent-flyer programme) in return for buying a certain amount of a particular product, rather than each time they purchase the goods. Random partial reinforcement is often used by cola drink manufacturers by etching letters on a certain quantity of their cans, leading to some purchasers receiving a prize.

Partial punishment is used when a basketball player has to leave the field for accumulating a certain number of fouls, whereas in football, players who foul are more likely to receive continuous punishment by being booked or sent off each time they commit an offence.

(d) **Passive and active avoidance:** In passive avoidance we avoid an aversive stimulus by not responding. For example, a child may refrain from fighting in the playground if he knows he will be punished. In active avoidance a child would actively avoid going to the playground in the first place, keeping away from a situation in which there is a possibility of fighting leading to further punishment.

(e) **Primary and secondary reinforcement:** Skinner differentiated between primary and secondary reinforcers. Primary reinforcers are basic reinforcers, usually fulfilling a physiological need like food, heat or light. When a rat receives food for pressing a lever, it primarily seeks the food, so reinforcing its behaviour. Secondary reinforcers on the other hand are learned reinforcers, usually from the social environment. For example, a child might associate her high chair (secondary reinforcer) with being fed (food as the primary reinforcer).

3.2.3 Evaluation

The Behaviourist approach to learning has had a wide influence. We can see simple, everyday stimulus-response learning behaviours all around us. How many times have we tried to screw off the cap of a bottle only to find that it is a flip top? How many times do we try to push a door open only to find we have to pull it towards us? In each case we have been conditioned one way and continue to apply our learning, not realising that such behaviour is inappropriate.

Many learning theorists (Coon, 1986), although accepting the great contributions of Pavlov and Skinner, have criticised the Behaviourist model as a whole. These criticisms include:

(a) **Ignoring human ability to learn:** The Behaviourist model excludes our ability to go beyond the situation and have independent and complex thoughts. It believes learning is rooted in conditioning.

(b) **Ignoring learner influence:** People differ in motivations, attitudes and emotions. The Behaviourist approach disregards these variables not only between individuals but also within people. For example, one day an individual's motivation may be high and learning will occur. The following day, the same individual may possess little or no motivation, so, regardless of the situation, the subject will not learn.

(c) **Dismisses individual differences:** Individuals' learning ability involves many variables, such as perceptions, past experiences, interests and motivations. Constant conditioning does not cancel them out.

(d) **Learning tends not to persist in the absence of reinforcement:** If rewards cease, it is more than likely behavioural responses (and therefore learning) also stop.

Behaviourist models are important within the framework of learning theories and we can see their many different applications. Their main opposition comes from an approach that analyses what happens within the 'head' rather than the reflexive behaviour of the subject. This is the Cognitive school of learning.

3.3 COGNITIVE LEARNING THEORIES

There are two main branches within the cognitive approach to learning: the **insight** approach and the **latent** approach. Superficially, they seem to have little in common, but the following descriptions will show that they are quite alike in assuming an organising principle that helps us to learn. While the Behaviourist school talked of S-R bonds, the cognitive theorists developed this to S-O-R bonds, through the use of an organising principle (O). The Cognitive theorists believe that learning involves higher mental processes and takes an almost information-processing, or problem-solving, approach to learning. We examine two models, insight learning and latent learning.

3.3.1 Insight learning

Wolfgang Kohler (1887-1968) was a member of the Gestalt school of psychology, who believed that the basis of learning was understanding the arrangement of the constituent parts of a situation. Further, that for learning truly to have taken place it was necessary to show that the skill/act/knowledge learnt was both repeatable and generalisable.

Kohler tried to discover whether apes could arrive at the solution to a problem according to the Gestalt principles already mentioned in section 2.4.2 above. He set the apes a problem: how to reach a bunch of bananas suspended from the top of their cage that they couldn't get to by climbing. Kohler provided the components of the solution by placing certain objects—boxes, chairs and sticks—at various locations in the cage.

Technically, the apes could solve the problem if they could manage to use each of the component parts of the solution (the boxes, the chairs and the sticks) *together*. After a number of unsuccessful attempts to reach the bananas by jumping or using the props individually, the chimps seemed to rest and contemplate.

Kohler   *Tolman*

Kohler's idea was that the apes could reach a solution if they could perceive the various composites of the problem within the same perceptual field. In the end, they were indeed able to use each of the props together and solve the problem.

Kohler observed the apes finding the solution in sudden eureka-like moment. That is, the apes had been puzzling over the solution for some time, but the answer came in a sudden burst of insight. In the same way, we may be trying to solve an anagram puzzle for a number of hours and suddenly realise what the solution is, in the way Ancient Greek mathematician Archimedes is said to have solved a scientific problem by seeing his bath water overflow and shouted, 'Eureka' (Greek for 'I've found it').

3.3.2 Latent learning

Latent learning, postulated by Edward C. Tolman, advances the idea that there is latent (or hidden) within us the ability to solve certain problems, though this may not be readily apparent in the learning situation.

Tolman based his theory on the outcome of experiments with rats. Essentially, Tolman placed rats in a maze to test their ability to learn the quickest way out. He split his test group in two and rewarded only one group with food on reaching the exit. He varied the solution to the problem, introducing obstacles into the maze, still rewarding only one of the two groups.

He found as time passed that the reward group were faster in finding the solution to the problem. However, after ten trials he began to reward the second group in an effort to see if they too would be able to find their way out of the maze as quickly as the group who had initially been rewarded. His hypothesis was supported. The second group now became as fast as the reward group in their ability to learn their way out of the maze.

Tolman suggested that, despite being rewarded only two thirds of the time, the ability to learn had been latent in the non-reward group and the reward triggered learning. During the non-reward time, the second group had been building up cognitive maps or internal representations of the maze (learning the layout) and, when necessary, could display the learning and be rewarded. Tolman said that individuals possess the ability to learn many skills, if the right stimulus is presented to bring those skills out.

3.3.3 Evaluation

Both cognitive models examined here have the notion of an organising principle supporting the learning process. The

Cognitive school sees learning as very much an individual process, influenced by such variables as motivation, perception and feedback.

Cognitive theorists agree that the role of memory is important in a learning situation, as it aids the process of thinking, storing and retrieving information. The main aspect of the Cognitive school's theories of learning is the idea that an 'organising', or reflective, principle is at work when we learn; we do not simply respond to stimuli.

3.3.4 Comparison of Behaviourist and Cognitive theories

(a)   **Stimulus-Response versus Stimulus-Organisation-Response**: Pavlov states that learning is merely a conditioning of responses and Skinner suggests learning is only the result of reinforcement. In other words, they are saying that memory is merely acquiring stimulus-response bonds, which can then be applied in particular situations. Kohler and Tolman believe that a person does not merely respond to a stimulus, and so learns, but actively organises the learning situation in order to process the stimuli, and so learns. This is how Stimulus-Organisation-Response bonds are acquired.

(b)   **The role of memory**: Memory is an important part of the learning process for Tolman, as it helped the rats in his experiment to learn the correct route when a reward was presented. For Pavlov, learning is merely the reflexive storage of facts, and experiences play no role.

(c)   **Individual differences**: The Cognitive school considers learning an individual process influenced by such variables as motivation, perception and feedback. The Behaviourists would refute this and say that we all learn in the same manner, irrespective of individual differences.

It could be argued that without our ability to retain and reflect on information, learning would not be possible. In the following section we move on to consider memory and the means by which we gain, store and use information.

3.4 MEMORY

Memory is an active system that receives, stores, organises, alters and recovers information.

3.4.1 Functions of memory

Memory has many uses in our lives. Although it is considered a hypothetical construct, it has multiple functions:

(a) **It records:** The memory provides a storage facility, ranging from specific personal episodes in our lives to the more general knowledge function providing a knowledge base from which we view our life situation and that of the world around us.

(b) **It organises and updates:** The memory arranges and rearranges our information, knowledge and feelings into compatible user states.

(c) **It learns:** Memory provides us with building blocks so that we can build up our knowledge.

(d) **It operates in the world:** The memory makes memories, recollections, learning experiences accessible when required.

To remember something, a person must be able to:

(a) **Encode:** To accept information in a usable form. In other words, information we wish to commit to memory must be entered in terms we understand, something like a computer programme. Unless we use the correct inputting programme, a computer will refuse to accept information. In our case, badly entered information will not be remembered correctly.

(b) **Store:** To be able to hold information in a certain way. We tend to store in line with our personal categorisation or reference system. For example, behavioural science information is stored in our memory apart from any other topic.

(c) **Retrieve:** It has the ability to recover information. This function is achieved only if the previous two stages are completed correctly, that information is entered in an understandable way and organised into specific categories.

Remembering is a complex phenomenon, widely studied by psychologists, yet questions concerning why we remember, how we remember and why we forget are still posed by lay people and psychologists alike.

For us to attempt to understand this phenomenon and offer tentative explanations of its workings, we must first address the question: What is memory? A general definition could be: 'the receiving, storing and retrieving of all types of sensory information'.

Many models of memory exist. We examine that of Atkinson & Shiffrin (1971).

3.4.2 Atkinson & Shiffrin model of memory

Atkinson and Shiffrin proposed a multi-store model of memory with three compartments working in harmony. Basically, information is received through the **sensory memory**. If we wish to retain the image or sound we pass it into the **short-term memory**, which in turn transfers the relevant information into the **long-term memory**, where it is stored for later use.

The following diagram is a simple model of what is described above. We describe the actions in each compartment in point form.

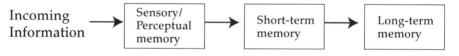

Sensory memory

(a)   Receives incoming information from the environment.

(b)   Holds an exact copy of what is seen or heard for up to two seconds.

(c)   Iconic (visual) memory lasts for approximately half a second.

(d)   Echoic (auditory) memory lasts for up to two seconds.

(d)   Holds information sufficiently long enough to facilitate transfer to the second compartment, short-term memory.

Short-term memory

(a)   Also referred to as working memory, it is the conscious process in which we deliberately attempt to memorise.

(b) Temporary storehouse containing only information that has been purposely selected.

(c) Needs rehearsal for retention. For example, if we are asked to remember a telephone number, we often keep repeating the digits until we can write the number down, or it has been transferred into long-term memory.

(d) Possesses a limited storage/duration capacity. Storage tends to be limited to 7+/-2 units of information, that is 5 to 9 units are the minimum and maximum storage limits. The limited duration capacity of short-term memory is 15 to 30 seconds.

(e) 'Chunking' occurs in short-term memory (Miller, 1956). We 'chunk' together items in an effort to make more space. For example, if you were asked to remember the following 12 words: *dog, brown, tall man, fence, lead, jump, the, his, took, to, above,* rather than individually remembering the words, which would fill up the short-term memory, a far better method is to make a sentence out of the words, converting the 12 units into one unit. Another chunking strategy is to 'pair' up words, again working on freeing up the short-term memory.

Long-term memory

(a) Information is transferred from short-term memory only if it is meaningful and makes sense.

(b) It has limitless capacity and duration. For example, we retain and accumulate memories from early childhood throughout our life.

(c) It tends to be an unconscious process (except for deliberate learning experiences), and rather complex. We are never quite sure why we remember a certain person's face, or a particular incident.

(d) Memories for iconic, echoic and motor movements reside here.

(e) It is often regarded as a permanent storehouse of memories.

3.4.3 Memory and forgetting

The study of forgetting has helped researchers to understand the nature of memory. If we know some of the reasons that memory does not operate successfully, we can deduce parts of its structure. The following are some suggested reasons for why we forget.

(a) **Retroactive inhibition**: Learning a new piece of information may interfere with previously held information on the same subject. For example, when a manufacturer brings out a new brand of washing powder, it may retroactively inhibit our memory of the older brand.

(b) **Proactive inhibition**: This is the opposite of the above. Namely, that previously held information inhibits retention of new information. For example, a friend's new telephone number might not be remembered because we were so used to the old number. The old number proactively inhibits the newer number.

(c) **Emotional factors**: If an individual is upset, memory for detail is poor. Courts, for example, are loath to convict solely on the basis of a victim's testimony, even though this may be the only evidence available. This is because the emotions of the time can interfere with the encoding process and the accuracy of recall. Conversely, marketing campaigns often attempt to evoke positive emotions in an audience to increase the likelihood of the consumer remembering the product. Humour used in adverts or the depiction of happy family life attempt to evoke positive emotions in the audience.

Improving memory

A number of strategies exist to improve memory, each placing strong emphasis on properly encoding information so that it can be effectively retrieved.

(a) **Mnemonics**: This is a device to aid memory by using combinations of letters which stand for the first letters of a number of other words and ideas, so minimising the amount of information and making it easier to learn. For example, if we were to try and learn the colours of the rainbow, we could construct the mnemonic **BOY GIVR**, which stands for:

Blue	**G**reen
Orange	**I**ndigo
Yellow	**V**iolet
	Red

The most commonly used memory aid for the colours of the

spectrum is either 'Richard of York Gave Battle In Vain' or 'Ring Out Your Great Bells In Victory'.

(b) **Regular rehearsal:** If we rehearse information regularly, we are more likely to remember. Most of us have little problem remembering our own phone number because we rehearse it so often. Researchers have shown that over 50 per cent of material which is not rehearsed is lost the next day.

(c) **Dependent learning:** Material is learned more effectively if it is retrieved in a similar situation to that in which it was learned, for example doing an examination in a quiet room should simulate the quiet conditions in which the study was done. Thus retrieval is dependent on the learning context.

This chapter has provided insight into an individual's learning behaviour. We have identified a wide variety of learning situations and the conditions that govern learning behaviour. We have, for example, shown that learning theorists do not speak with one voice about the role of incentives, rewards or punishments, and that there is much disagreement about the importance and practice of understanding and insight into the learning process. Nevertheless, despite differences, the various approaches provide the reader with an overall view of an individual's learning environment.

3.5 SUMMARY

1. The two main theories of learning are the Behaviourist approach and the Cognitive approach.

2. The Behaviourist approach consists of classical conditioning (Pavlov), emphasising the role of association in learning, and operant conditioning (Skinner), emphasising the importance of positive and negative reinforcement.

3. The Cognitive approach to learning includes the insight (Kohler) and the latent (Tolman) approaches.

4. The insight approach suggests that the successful solution of a problem depends on the arrangement of that problem in the perceiver's mind, while the latent approach suggests we have a

3.5 SUMMARY CONTD.

latent ability to learn which manifests itself when certain 'rewards' are presented.

5. Memory consists of three stages—sensory, short-term memory and long-term memory—each possessing its own distinctive attributes.

3.6 EXAM QUESTIONS

1. How would training programmes based on classical versus operant conditioning differ?

2. Distinguish between the Cognitive and Behaviourist approaches to learning. Give examples of each in your answer.

3. Recommend strategies for improving recall of study material based on Atkinson and Shiffrin's model of memory.

4. What are the major stages of memory? Suggest some reasons why we forget.

5. Pick one suitable advertisement or marketing promotion and outline how it draws on Behaviourist learning principles.

Chapter 4

Motivation

Motivation concerns what drives a person's
choice of what to do, how hard to try,
and how long to keep trying.

Arnold, Cooper and Robertson (1998)

4

Motivation

Learning objectives

After studying this chapter, you should be able to:

1. *Understand the differing definitions of motivation, and distinguish between motives, drives and needs.*

2. *Describe and explain responses to frustration.*

3. *Explain the Content theorists approach to motivation.*

4. *Explain the Process theorists approach to motivation.*

5. *Describe motivation research methodologies.*

4.1 INTRODUCTION

Motivation is a multi-faceted concept. The complex and pervasive nature of ideas about motivation can sometimes lead to ambiguities in our understanding of the concept. In one sense, motives are a particular class of reasons for doing something—as in a motive for murder. In another broader sense, motive is a term we use to describe the strength of someone's impulse to action, for example when we speak of someone being strongly motivated to achieve.

From a psychological perspective we are interested in the second wider understanding of the term. We use as a starting point that individuals are active and that this activity is instigated by having both a discernible direction (goal-seeking) and a measure of intensity (pursuing goals with persistence). How such goal-directed behaviour is instigated derives from an interaction between internal states and external stimulation.

We begin with a look at the various terms involved in motivation, describing their interrelationship and examining what happens when motivation is hampered or obstructed, or how we respond to frustration. We then move on to the various approaches to, and theories of, motivation.

It is important to note that any theory is not airtight, as all theories have strengths and limitations. What we offer is a selection of the main theories of motivation divided into the Content and Process models. First, we need to address the many concepts and definitions, which arise from a study of motivation.

Motivation: basic and associated concepts

When the Olympics come around there is a spate of programmes on the athletes' build-up to the games, showing how preparation and training takes its toll financially and emotionally. We ask how they can push themselves to such extremes of mental and physical endurance? Is it to pursue excellence or to attain glory? Both of these terms are accepted motives in this setting. We are questioning the role of motivation in their lives.

Motivation plays an important part in achievement.

In studying motivation, we attempt to answer such questions as:

(a)   Why do some people seem more driven than others?

(b)   Can this difference be attributed to environment or upbringing? If it is the latter, can we influence the level of motivation in individuals?

(c)   How much does the situation in which we find ourselves affect our level of motivation?

(d)   Is it hard to motivate workers or potential consumers?

The study of motivation is important because of its psychological implications for human behaviour. Knowledge of motivational components can help us to gain a better insight into the 'why' of human behaviour.

What is motivation?

A definition of motivation necessitates a definition of the terms 'drives' and 'needs'. It may help to illustrate this with an example. On a warm summer's day we feel thirsty. Once we realise this, we decide to look for a shop where we can buy something thirst-quenching. The thirst we feel is the **need**, our **motive** is to find a shop, and the strength of our need for liquid determines the strength of our **drive** to find a shop. If the need is strong enough, the drive will be correspondingly strong.

Many definitions of motivation exist. Arnold, Cooper and Robertson (1998) offer the following description of motivation: 'Motivation concerns what drives a person's choice of what to do, how hard to try, and how long to keep trying. It is *not* the only factor which influences work performance.' In other words, motivation is a driving force that impels people into action.

Perhaps at a physiological level this is an adequate explanation, such as an extreme thirst driving us to find a drink. The issue becomes more complex when we consider the variety of psychological factors involved in people's choices in relation to drives. For example you may be thirsty, but do you buy a bottle of water, cola or beer? Your choice is dependent on a number of factors; your age, preferences, and situational factors (many shops don't stock beer) to mention a few. Similarly, as Arnold *et al.* (1998) highlight, motivation alone does not determine work performance. Performance is influenced by many other situational variables, such as organisational culture, resources or training provided.

4.2 STATE AND TRAIT MOTIVATION

State motivation refers to the acquisition of a motive (of varying strength) from the particular state or situation you find yourself in. Returning to the Olympic athletes, they would experience state motivation when competing on the day, due to the atmosphere of the stadium and the presence of the fans. The whole sense of occasion would contribute to their motivational state. Similarly your 'need' for liquid might be satisfied in a different way while on a hike as opposed to in a pub with your friends.

The difference between people in terms of strength of drives, is called trait motivation. The strength of an individual's motivation is not a function of the situation in which people find themselves but is dependent on the strength of their inherent motivational trait.

In sport, it is often not the person with the greater natural ability who wins, but the one who is more driven. A sports writer summed this up when comparing two different types of footballers: 'Good players are *often* highly motivated, the best are *always* highly motivated.'

McClelland (1961) has written extensively about this particular type of motivation, which we shall examine later in this chapter. First, there are a number of important concepts to analyse before we examine a selection of motivational theorists offering varied and challenging motivational frameworks.

4.3 DRIVES

Drives are powerful motivating forces necessary for survival purposes. There is a distinction between learned and unlearned drives.

4.3.1 Unlearned and learned drives

Unlearned drives are innate and relate to our physiological survival. They include hunger, thirst and sleep. From the moment we are born, we strive for fulfilment of these needs. While we can go for months without food, we cannot go without water or sleep for more than a few days. When the balance between these internal needs is upset, the body reacts by experiencing drives to satisfy these needs. The balance we return to is known as **homeostasis**. Because drives are unlearned, primary and physiological in nature, regardless of individual or societal differences, all individuals experience similar sensations.

Learned drives, on the other hand, are social in nature and acquired by the socialisation process. Learned drives may take the form of needing to make friends, establishing sexual relationships and learning what role is expected of us in society, and expressing a drive to achieve it. The nature and extent of these drives is learned and may be affected by such things as parental style, the culture in which we find ourselves and personality factors.

Whereas every human experiences the physiological needs described above, there may be enormous individual differences in terms of learned drives. For example, individuals differ in their needs for social companionship and for approval.

4.3.2 Positive and negative drives

Positive drives motivate us to achieve a positive outcome, such as an increase in our salary or getting top marks in an exam. Advertisers attempt to portray the acquisition of their products in terms of a positive drive trying to convince consumers they will feel good once the product is bought.

Negative drives motivate us to avoid unpleasant outcomes. For example, a student facing a school test plays truant for the day. Advertisers try to persuade us to buy various types of toothbrushes or toothpastes on the grounds that we will avoid dental problems by using them.

The concept of drives offers the following combinations:

(a) **Positive learned drives**   Wanting to meet people, having a successful career.

(b) **Positive unlearned drives**   Wanting to eat and drink when we are hungry.

(ci) **Negative learned drives**   Wanting to avoid a visit to the dentist or the doctor.

(d) **Negative unlearned drives**   Wanting to avoid pain, for example when we put our hand too close to a fire we pull it away quickly and instinctively when we start to feel the pain.

4.4 RESPONSES TO FRUSTRATION

In examining motivation one must investigate not just how individuals perform in optimum conditions, but also how they react to obstacles and frustrations. The study of responses to frustration enhances the study of motivation and can show us the power of the frustrated drive. The level of frustration we feel is often related to the strength of the drive; for example, if we had worked ten hours a day over a year to do well in an exam and had only gained a pass mark, we would be very disappointed and frustrated.

The following are some ways in which the psychoanalyst Sigmund Freud suggested we respond to frustration. These are known as defence mechanisms:

(a) **Compensation**: We often attempt to 'make it up' to ourselves for a failure or disappointment. For example, if an individual is frustrated in an attempt to attain an executive position in a local tennis club, the person may compensate for this by working harder in her career in order to derive a sense of achievement.

(b) **Regression**: When behaviour is thwarted, we may find it difficult to cope with the consequences and we regress or return to previously experienced secure states or modes of behaviour. Children often display regressive behaviour, such as thumb-sucking, when disciplined by parents.

(c) **Repression**: When denied the opportunity to fulfil a strongly desired goal, the desire to achieve may be repressed. This is effectively a form of denial, which seeks to shut out from the individual's conscious mind the fact that the goal could not be attained.

(d) **Projection**: We often realise some of our drives are socially unacceptable and so we may avoid this realisation by ascribing these views to others. Some people like soap operas but feel it is socially unacceptable to admit it so they project this 'liking' onto others.

(e) **Problem-solving behaviour**: When we experience frustration, we may decide on alternative ways of achieving a goal. For example, roadworks can prevent us from travelling a particular route, so we select an alternative rather than be annoyed with the situation.

(f) **Apathy**: We may simply give up and do nothing rather than choosing to react.

(g) **Aggression**: Aggression can take a number of forms:

   (i) **Constructive**, whereby we redouble our efforts to achieve a particular goal, as a rugby team tries doubly hard when held up at the goal line of their opponents.

(ii) **Destructive**, which aims to eliminate the persons or obstacles that impede the achievement of a goal. This is negative by its very nature. In the rugby example this might involve: the team using foul play to try and cross the line (direct destructive behaviour), or after leaving the field, being rude to their trainer (indirect destructive behaviour). Workers who experience difficulty in the workplace and take out their frustrations on their spouse and family use indirect destructive behaviour.

(h) **Rationalisation**: If we fail to obtain a job, we often rationalise this frustration in terms of interviewer bias.

Having dealt with a general overview of the term motivation, we now proceed to examine specific theories of motivation.

4.5 TRADITIONAL MOTIVATIONAL THEORY

4.5.1 F.W. Taylor

F.W. Taylor (1856-1915) is considered the founder of scientific management principles and the most significant theorist under the banner of traditional management theories. His 'Principles of Scientific Management' were adopted within many organisations, setting the framework for what became known as job specialisation.

Briefly, Taylor's distinct phases are:

(a) Identification of task and employment of a team.

(b) Task analysis and job specialisation.

(c) Task assignment and training.

(d) Continued supervision, co-ordination and planning.

Taylor felt that only when a secure, tightly controlled framework was in place (providing employees with strict guidelines) could motivation be encouraged. He put forward the notion that money was a prime motivator of work performance, with workers responding to the offer of more money by working proportionately harder (Taylor, 1947).

He tested his theories on a railway worker called Schmidt (Taylor, 1947), whose job it was to load iron onto trains. The average amount of iron loaded per day by the 75 workers at the depot was 12.5 tons. Taylor calculated that with the right incentive he could get Schmidt to load between 47 and 48 tons per day. He offered Schmidt a bonus depending on how much he loaded, and observed him over a period of three years. Taylor noted a significant improvement in performance, to 47 tons per day. Taylor's views are widespread, particularly amongst employers.

The obvious conclusion is that given the right monetary incentive, workers will work harder with little or no reference to issues such as how they are made feel in their jobs, working conditions, or respect from management. A further implication is that workers can work harder, but will only do so for extra money. Many employers have taken this to mean that workers are lazy or that they are trying to get paid as much as they possibly can, before being as productive as they can.

It should be remembered that:

(a)   Taylor framed his theory of scientific management when labour was cheap, the workforce badly paid and operating in primitive working conditions. Set against this background, it is easy to see how the workforce, would be so motivated by money.

(b)   Schmidt, being muscular, was exceptionally well suited to a labourer's job. Others may not be as well suited physically or mentally to their jobs and so may not be able to improve their performance as significantly.

(c)   Taylor's ideas were controversial even at the time they were introduced. The reduction in employee numbers due to scientific management led to tense industrial relations at the steelworks where Taylor acted as a consultant.

4.6 CONTENT THEORIES OF MOTIVATION

Content or Need theories place emphasis on what actually motivates the worker or ordinary person. They identify what workers need, the strength of the needs and how workers will behave in order to satisfy these needs. We examine the following Content or Need theorists:

(a)   Abraham Maslow.

(b)   David C. McClelland.

(c)   Douglas McGregor.

(d)   Frederick Herzberg.

The first of these is perhaps the best known. His work is often remembered for the diagrams it has produced namely Maslow's hierarchy of needs.

4.6.1 Maslow's Hierarchy of Needs

Abraham Maslow's work centred on the belief that our needs are hierarchical in nature: certain basic needs such as hunger and thirst have to be fulfilled before the individual could contemplate moving on to fulfil other higher order needs, such as a need for self-esteem.

The famous hierarchy, represented in a pyramidic fashion, contains an individual's progressive needs (which appear from the bottom up on the pyramid).

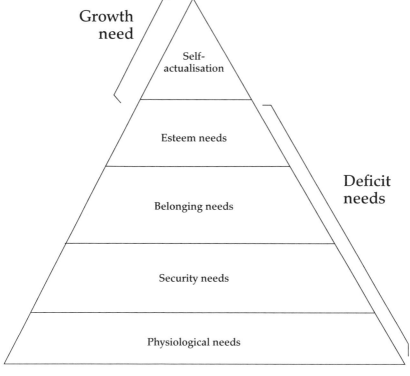

Maslow's Hierarchy of Needs

Deficit and growth needs

The bottom four levels on the hierarchy are termed the **deficit** needs. The top one, the **growth** need, is so called because without the others we experience social and physiological deficits without which we would not grow.

(a) **Physiological needs:** These are our basic needs, such as hunger, thirst and sleep. They are unlearned and must be satisfied before we can think about satisfying any other types of drive.

(b) **Security needs:** Most people crave a structure in their lives. They have learned security needs, such as order and stability, which find expression in terms of law and order and a sense of personal security. Citizens in newly emerging countries are often concerned with establishing an ordered society.

(c) **Belonging needs:** These refer to learned social needs, finding expression in the need for love, affection and affiliation. Most societies provide an opportunity for their citizens to seek fulfilment of these belonging needs.

(d) **Esteem needs:** As learned social needs, esteem needs have to do with the need for appreciation from peers, symbolising the need for prestige and success. Usually, this need finds expression in our working lives, where a high salary can often engender respect and admiration from those around us.

(e) **Self-actualisation:** Probably a minority of people realise their true potential. In other words they do not self-actualise. Most people do not self-actualise because they are unable to, do not feel themselves able to, or are not in a position to take the road to self-discovery.

According to Maslow, we must fulfil one set of needs before we can, or would want to, embark on fulfilling the next set. For example, individuals trying to fulfil the needs on the first rung of the hierarchy are not interested in self-esteem needs or self-actualising needs.

Drawing on Maslow's work, Alderfer posited the existence of a simpler model of three needs called ERG theory. These he called existence (E), relatedness (R) and growth (G) needs, which could be satisfied in any order. Existence needs relate to Maslow's physiological and security levels, relatedness to the belonging level and growth to esteem and self-actualisation needs. Furnham (1997) claims that Alderfer's theory provides a better fit with available research evidence, which suggests that although types of need exist they do not conform to the strict hierarchical model proposed by Maslow.

It is interesting to note how organisational theorists have adapted Maslow's hierarchy in terms of employee fulfilment:

Growth need

Responsibility, working and being rewarded.

Status, job titles, company car and bonus schemes.

Sense of place and role in the company. Social avenues.

Permanent contract with pension. Job design.

Job and salary.

Deficit needs

A version of Maslow's hierarchy adapted for organisations

Maslow's hierarchy is also used from a marketing perspective, where marketing campaigns address each section of needs as being met by that product. For example, buying 'Beauty' soap will fulfil needs as follows:

(a) It will keep you clean. (Physiological needs)

(b) It has long-lasting effects. (Security needs)

(c)   Only those people who care about their skin buy this product. (Belonging needs)

(d)   Only the most discerning and youthful-looking people buy this product. (Self-esteem)

(e)   If you buy this, who knows what it might lead to! (Self-actualisation)

From both an organisational and marketing viewpoint, it is not strictly necessary to target each rung in the ladder (although a Maslow purist would disagree). Often a manager may try to fulfil only an employee's security needs, while a marketing campaign might target the self-esteem needs.

4.6.2 McClelland's Need Theory

David C. McClelland also believed individuals are motivated by need fulfilment. However his theoretical framework encompasses only three needs:

(a)   Need for power.

(b)   Need for affiliation.

(c)   Need for achievement.

It is the third need that we are going to look at, as McClelland believed 'need for achievement' was the strongest and denoted an individual's level of motivation. To see exactly what McClelland means by need for achievement, we must examine where exactly he places its genesis.

McClelland suggested that there are two ways in which need for achievement develops:

(i)   **Parental style:** McClelland states that our parents may imbue us with a positive attitude towards work and success. They may instil within us a desire to succeed, which transfers itself into a need, which in turn motivates us towards fulfilling and thus achieving behaviour.

(ii) **Country of origin:** McClelland suggested that those who came from what were regarded as predominantly Protestant countries were more likely to display high need for achievement. He felt they had incorporated a Protestant 'work ethic' into their culture, which affected every level of their society. McClelland (1961) attempted to support his assertions by pointing to the significantly greater amount of kilowatt-hours consumed by factories in Protestant countries, as opposed to non-Protestant countries, thus supposedly displaying greater industriousness on the part of the former.

McClelland also stated that those individuals displaying higher need for achievement were more likely to be engaged in enterprise, to be entrepreneurs. Further research has suggested however that high need for achievement is not solely restricted to the entrepreneurial field, it also includes areas such as sport and politics. The common denominator between these areas, however, is that all the participants have to have a great deal of motivation to succeed.

From his studies, McClelland suggested that those who have high need for achievement display the following traits:

(a) A preference for **working by themselves**, rather than having to submit themselves to the dictates of a superior. Personal responsibility is something desired by those displaying high need for achievement.

(b) They set themselves **moderate goals**, which are more realistic and have more chance of success.

(c) They are **realistic** and **seek out information** on their situation. This helps them to set the moderate goals mentioned in the last point.

(d) They appreciate **regular feedback** on their activities.

The following diagram illustrates this relationship.

We turn next to theorists who have concentrated on the area of work and organisational motivation. These theorists are important because their ideas and beliefs are still influential today.

4.6.3 McGregor's Theory X and Theory Y

Douglas McGregor, a need theorist similar to Maslow and McClelland, believed that motivation was obtained through fulfilment of employee needs. He disagreed with Taylorism, the traditional view of management, stating it had a very negative viewpoint of the worker as it ignored workers' needs for fulfilment and described them as lazy, indolent and solely motivated by threats, punishment or monetary incentives. McGregor realised this picture of the employee was one adopted by many organisations. He named it Theory X.

Recognising that employees had needs such as self-fulfilment and responsibility, McGregor (1960) proposed a different view, labelled Theory Y. This conceptualises the worker as someone who actively seeks self-fulfilment from their job and seeks direction from others in how to do so. It further asserts that each worker is willing to take on more responsibility in an effort to solve problems within the organisation.

Many organisations employ Theory Y in their treatment of workers, by investing in human resource management (HRM), giving employees facilities not dependent upon increased productivity and employing less rigid management structures. Proponents of Theory Y recognise and offer workers increased responsibility; for example, by appointing worker directors and by soliciting the views of workers through suggestion boxes.

4.6.4 Herzberg's Two Factor Theory

Motivational theorist Frederick Herzberg, working in the late 1950s and early 1960s, recognised the value of need theories within organisational life. He developed the Two Factor Theory of motivation, so called because he recognised two separate sets of factors affecting work motivations.

His research involved using the Critical Incident Technique, where 200 engineers and accountants were asked to relate work incidents in which they felt particularly good or bad about their jobs. Responses clearly defined two sets of factors, satisfiers (motivating factors) and dissatisfiers (hygiene factors).

Hygiene factors are not so much motivational factors as maintenance factors. In other words, if any of these are absent, dissatisfaction will follow. If they are present, employees will experience neither dissatisfaction nor motivation, and be merely 'satisfied' with their job. These factors preventing dissatisfaction, called dissatisfiers, do not promote motivation. If workers are unhappy with basic aspects of their jobs such as salary, work conditions, interpersonal relationships and security, it can produce dissatisfaction and lead to industrial disputes.

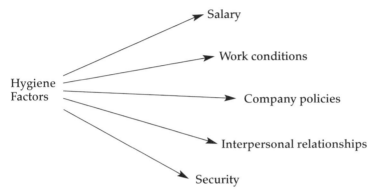

Hygiene factors in an organisation

On the other hand, workers can be motivated to enhance their performance by what Herzberg (1959, 1974) termed 'motivating factors', such as responsibility, personal advancement and a sense of achievement. An employer does not have to supply these, but if they are present they will lead to greater employee satisfaction and motivation, and therefore they are known as satisfiers.

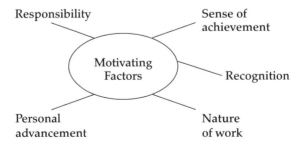

*The factors that actually motivate employees
towards increased performance levels.*

Note that hygiene factors tend to involve factors related to the work environment, while the motivating factors tend to involve job content.

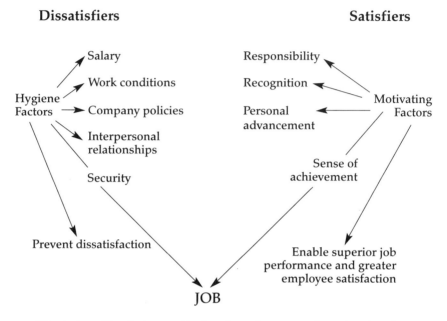

Dissatisfiers   **Satisfiers**

The interaction between the hygiene factors and motivating factors

Herzberg's theory makes three assumptions, that:

(a) Employees are not motivated by monetary reward.

(b) Employees require job content and motivators to experience satisfaction.

(c) The absence of hygiene factors leads to dissatisfaction only.

4.7 PROCESS THEORIES OF MOTIVATION

Where Content theorists identified and focussed on **what** motivated the worker, Process theorists believe that motivation is actually a dynamic process of initiating and directing behaviours. In this section, we deal with two process theorists:

(a) Victor Vroom.

(b) J. Stacey Adams.

4.7.1 Vroom and Expectancy Theory

Vroom proposed a model of motivation based on three variables: valence, instrumentality and expectancy. The theory as a whole is based on the supposition that workers prefer a favourable to a less favourable outcome and will become motivated to ensure the former. Favourability is the result of the interaction of instrumentality, valence and expectancy:

(a) **Valence:** If a person is attracted to a particular outcome, it possesses a positive valence (e.g. +1), whereas if he is negative about the result, it possesses a negative valence (e.g. -1). If indifferent towards the outcome, a zero valence is recognised. The three states above might correspond to achieving a salary increase, being asked to do overtime, or the suggestion that the worker's offices be painted in a pastel colour.

(b) **Instrumentality:** In this, Vroom distinguished between first-level outcomes (which are performance-related) and second-level outcomes (which are need-related). Vroom suggested that the extent to which workers attempt first-level outcomes is a result of how important the second-level outcome is to them, and the probability that first level outcomes will lead to second-level outcomes. The prospect of a pay increase (second-level outcome) may motivate us highly in our work (first-level outcome). It is the strength of the linkage between the first- and second-level outcomes that determines their effectiveness. In this respect, they can be rated from +1 (strong linkage) to -1 (weak linkage).

(c) **Expectancy:** This is the extent to which the person being motivated believes that there is a chance or probability of a particular outcome. This could be the probability that the managing director will provide a place on the board. If the worker does not believe that this will happen, this affects her motivation accordingly. Expectancy can range from 0 (that there is no chance of the event happening) to 1 (indicating certainty that a particular outcome will be reached).

Vroom suggested that the above can be framed in the following equation. In this equation F stands for the force of your motivation, which is a function of the sum of (Σ) valences (V), times the instrumentality (I), times the strength of the expectancies (E):

$$F = \Sigma \, (V \times I \times E)$$

An example of Vroom's theory can be seen in the following activity, from Buchanan and Huczynski (1991):

First: List the outcomes that you expect will result from working hard for your present course, such as:
(a)   High exam marks.
(b)   Bare pass.
(c)   Sleepless nights.
(d)   No social life.

Second: Rate the value you place on each of these outcomes, giving those you like +1, those you dislike -1, and those for which you are neutral 0. These are your V values.

Third: Analyse the linkage between first-level and second-level outcomes, for example what is the probability that working long hours (first-level outcome) will lead to high exam marks (second-level outcome)? This can range from +1 (strong linkage) to -1 (weak linkage). These are your I values.

Fourth: Estimate the probability of attaining each of these outcomes, giving those that are certain the value 1, those that are most unlikely the value 0, and those for which there is an even chance the value 0.5. Estimate other probabilities as you perceive them at other values between 0 and 1. These are your E values.

Fifth: Now put your I, E and V values into the expectancy equation:

$$F = \sum (V \times I \times E)$$

and add up the result.

Sixth: Compare your F score with the scores of your colleagues. We predict that:

-   Those with higher scores are the course 'swots'.
-   Those with the higher scores will get higher exam marks.

While well framed, Vroom's theory has not received strong empirical support (Galbraith and Cummings, 1967), though the same research showed (somewhat like Mayo's findings in the Hawthorne studies) that the valence of workers' duties increased when they perceived that the instrumentality of attention (from their supervisors) increased. In other words, they worked harder if they felt they would receive more attention from their supervisors.

4.7.2 Adams and Equity Theory

Adams suggested that worker satisfaction is a result of achieving equity between their inputs (effort, training, ability) and their outputs (salary, status, and job benefits) as illustrated by the diagram below. Perceived inequity may be a result of a perceived disparity in the ratio of inputs to outputs, not just that the inputs outweigh the outputs. To arrive at this conclusion, Adams suggests that workers actively compare their lot with those in a similar position. The inequity is not just a function of their own inputs and outputs, but also how they perceive the equity or inequity of those in a similar position to themselves.

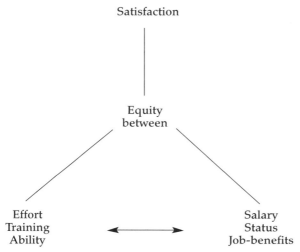

Worker satisfaction comes from equity between inputs and outputs.

There are a number of ways that employees can react to perceived inequity (as outlined in Mullins, 1999):

(a) **Changes to inputs:** A person may adjust the level of their inputs, either up or down, to match their outcome. They may, for instance, decide to do less overtime, agree to take a pay reduction or demotion, or try to improve the quality of their work.

(b) **Changes to outcomes:** A person may attempt to change their outcomes, such as pay and working conditions, without changes to inputs. This is often the case in Irish industrial relations where workers frequently believe they should be paid more or should work a reduced working week.

(c) **Cognitive distortion of inputs and outcomes:** People may distort—in their own mind—their inputs and outcomes so as to achieve a perceived level of equity, for example they may convince themselves that they are more qualified and another person is working less than they are.

(d) **Acting on others:** A person may try and get others to accept different inputs (work harder or less hard), outcomes (accept less salary or less promotion); and they may try to force others to leave the work situation.

(e) **Changing the object of comparison:** People may try to change the reference point, so as to compare themselves with those they feel they would be achieving equity with. They may do this by convincing themselves that the people they are initially being compared with have moved into a different, higher, category and so there is no inequity.

(f) **Leaving the field:** A person may try and leave the inequitable situation they find themselves in, by moving for example.

In recent years a number of disputes have arisen in sectors such as education and health care due to the perception amongst teachers and nurses that their inputs and outcomes were inequitable. Many workers' demands centred on the perceived inequity of their pay, as compared with other workers in similar sectors.

4.8 MOTIVATION RESEARCH

Even though the majority of motivation research carried out nowadays is in the area of marketing (why consumers buy particular products), it originated in the field of psychology. This is an important point as some researchers feel that its involvement in the field of marketing has produced a one-dimensional theory of people's motivations, only as consumers.

We shall look at some of the ways in which we may examine people's motivations. These tests are in the main derived from clinical psychology and are usually of a projective nature. This means that individuals are not called on to state explicitly what their feelings are on a particular issue, but rather reveal them by how they respond to certain test cues with which they are presented:

(a) **Thematic Apperception Test (TAT):** The person is shown a drawing or photograph and asked to make up a story about it. For example, in the TAT—which can measure need for achievement—people are presented with a picture of an executive in an office looking at a picture of her husband and children. High need for achievement responses to this stimulus would emphasise a strongly driven executive, supported and encouraged by her family. Low need for achievement response would include emphasis on the executive's loneliness in her work environment, away from a family whom she misses.

(b) **Rorschach test:** In what is more commonly known as the 'ink blot' test, a person is presented with a number of brightly coloured ink-blot shapes and asked to reply spontaneously as to what he thinks the ink blots look like. The test examines imagination, originality and variety of thoughts. It can often be useful in examining deep-seated feelings and emotions. A variation is used in marketing research when a consumer is asked for spontaneous reactions to new designs for packaging.

(c) **Word association test:** Developed by the psychiatrist Carl Gustav Jung, this test presents the person with single words asking her to respond with the first word that enters her head. It is designed to examine the mental associations an individual possesses, in a quick, easily accessible manner. This can also be used in a marketing sphere to test what consumers think about a new product.

(d) **Research questionnaire:** This is one of the primary instruments used by all researchers to test attitudes. It may be administered in person, on the street or in the home, or it can be sent through the post. It can be a very powerful tool in quantifying the strength and magnitude of individuals' feelings towards products, social issues or services.

An understanding of motivation is important in understanding actions in all spheres of life. Study of the topic provides insights into how exactly people are motivated or how it is possible to accommodate people's needs and expectations. We have also seen here that workers are not motivated to work harder purely by the offer of more money, but rather by complex factors such as how they are respected by their workmates and supervisors.

4.9 SUMMARY

1. Motivation is the interrelationship between needs, behaviour aimed at overcoming and fulfilling needs and the fulfilment of these needs, and is a driving force that impels people into action.

2. Drives are powerful motivating forces, which impel us towards realising needs. The perceived importance and strength of needs vary from person to person.

3. Responses to frustration can often be in the form of defence mechanisms, such as problem-solving, aggression and rationalisation.

4. Theories of motivation are divided into Need or Content theorists, including Maslow, McClelland, Herzberg and McGregor, and Process theorists Vroom and Adams.

5. Common research methods into motivation include the TAT, the Rorschach test, Jung's word association test and the research questionnaire.

4.10 EXAM QUESTIONS

1. What lessons could either (a) a manager interested in motivating employees; or (b) a marketing executive planning an advertising campaign, learn from theories of motivation?

2. Describe the assumptions about human nature underpinning McGregor's Theory X and Y.

3. Explain the main aspects of McClelland's theory of motivation. In your opinion does it present a credible theory of what motivates human beings?

4. Describe the main ways in which we react to being frustrated. In your answer you should provide examples of each of the coping mechanisms you present.

5. Examine the main similarities and differences between need and process theories of motivation.

Chapter 5

Attitudes

When one maintains his proper attitude in life,
he does not long after externals.

Epictetus (A.D. c.50-c.138)

5

Attitudes

Learning objectives

After studying this chapter, you should be able to:

1. *Understand the major definitions of attitudes.*

2. *Describe the characteristics, components, functions and sources of attitudes.*

3. *Understand the major attitudinal measurement scales.*

4. *Discuss consistency models of attitudes.*

5. *Explain and evaluate the variables concerned with attitude change.*

5.1 INTRODUCTION

The attitudes we hold affect most aspects of our lives: our behaviours, opinions, friendships, motives and learning. Attitudes are basically how we feel about something. A knowledge of attitudes is important if we wish to understand human behaviour. If we gain insight into how and why attitudes are formed we may understand others' views and actions. Attitudes often indicate how we feel about something: for example, attitudes towards authority, towards social issues, towards responsibility.

The difficulty with studying attitudes is that (as with so many psychological topics) it is a hypothetical construct and therefore unseen, so we have to infer the presence of an attitude from a person's behaviour—unless the person chooses to supplement their behaviour with a report of their attitudes.

Within organisational spheres, attitudes will frequently determine the general approach of an employee to work—in terms of conscientiousness, motivation or responsibility. In marketing, whenever consumers are asked to express their feelings about a product or service, they are being asked to express their attitudes.

In this chapter we examine a number of aspects of attitudes. For example, what they consist of, how they are acquired, and what actions they serve. We also introduce a number of attitudinal models and methodologies developed by behavioural scientists in an effort to measure attitudes.

5.2 ATTITUDES - POSSIBLE DEFINITIONS

Researchers have dedicated a large amount of research in attempting a definition of attitudes, in order to differentiate it from things such as views and beliefs, and other cognitive processes. The following are a sample of the definitions on this topic.

Krech and Crutchfield (1948) defined an attitude as 'an enduring organisation of motivational, emotional, perceptual and cognitive processes with respect to some aspect of the individual's world'. They described an attitude as a wide umbrella of interactions towards the world, embracing feelings such as sadness, motivation and happiness.

Gordon Allport (1954) defined an attitude as 'a mental and neural state of readiness, organised through experience, exerting a directive or dynamic influence upon the individual's response to all situations and situations with which it is related'. Allport describes an attitude as a dynamic force, involving interactions with the outside world. This approach differs slightly from Krech and Crutchfield's in that Allport views us as being ready at all times to express our attitudes by what we do and say.

Krech, Crutchfield and Ballachey (1962) later defined an attitude as 'an enduring system of positive or negative evaluations, emotional feeling and pro or con action states towards a social object'. This seeks to narrow the range of attitudes to those within our social sphere.

Eagly and Chaiken (1993) define attitudes as 'tendencies to evaluate an entity into some degree of favour or disfavour, ordinarily expressed in cognitive, affective, and behavioural responses'. We will see below that this definition—by including cognitive, affective, and behavioural responses—seeks to accommodate the main attitudinal theories, particularly the tri-component model.

An attitude is a somewhat complex phenomenon, involving factors such as **beliefs**, where we accept something is true, for example statements about relationships ('I have a good employer'), and **values** which are special types of beliefs, often expressed as an abstract ideal ('I think marriage is a sacred institution'); an ideal mode of conduct (for example, honesty and loyalty) and ideal goals (for example, happiness, equality and security).

Our attitude towards divorce, for example, may be an interaction of our belief system (belief in the strength of the family unit) and value system (fidelity and loyalty are important tenets in all human relationships). Naturally, our past experiences, environment and important 'others' in our lives affect how we feel towards any particular object or situation.

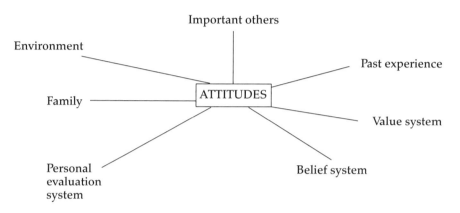

Attitudes embrace many different factors.

Put simply, an attitude is an inclination to perceive, interpret and evaluate people, events and issues in a certain manner.

5.2.1 Characteristics of an attitude

Attitudes have several important characteristics:

(a) **They are learned**: We are not born with attitudes; we learn them primarily from the family (our first socialising group) and from society at large. Some psychologists suggest that the large increase in the incidence of anorexia nervosa amongst young women is as a result of idealised images of very thin women being shown regularly in the media. In turn, this leads to young women believing that this is the correct attitude towards their body, which leads to abnormal eating patterns to achieve this weight.

(b) **They are persistent**: Unlike a mood, attitudes will persist over time. We see evidence of this in Iran's attitude towards the writer Salman Rushdie, who wrote a book that offended the leaders of the country. The intensity of their negative attitude has not wavered over the years. Animal-rights activists tend not to become meat-eating supporters of fox hunting overnight.

(c) **They are predictive of behaviour:** Because an attitude expresses how someone feels, we can use this as a measure of behavioural predictability. Opinions on this differ; some psychologists believe attitudes only suggest a general pattern of behaviour rather than specific, predictable actions.

For marketers, the ability to predict whether an attitude will lead to buying specific brands is essential in deciding budgets and a marketing strategy. If market research shows that certain attitudes lead to particular behaviour, marketers feel justified in sanctioning expenditure on advertising in certain media. For example, they might feel that vegetarians would be more likely to buy non-GMO (genetically modified organism) food, as they have shown by their attitudes that they were interested in unadulterated foodstuffs that do not affect the environment so much.

(d) **They can exist at low levels of consciousness:** Frequently, an individual may be unaware of how strongly they feel towards a situation until a discussion is entered into, or they are required to vote or make an input into a topic. We might, for example, not have been very concerned about the debate about whether or not parents should slap their children. But when presented with a public example of this behaviour, we might find it upsetting and we might intervene with the parent carrying it out.

(e) **They retain the uniqueness of human experience:** The individuality of the person plays a big part in expression of attitudes. Many people may share a similar attitude, but expression and/or behaviour related to an attitude may differ simply because of the uniqueness of their experience. This happened in Ireland when many members of the same family, all committed to Irish independence, fought on opposite sides in the Civil War. Another example could be of friends who have the same attitude towards fashion and style choosing different clothes.

5.3 FUNCTIONS OF ATTITUDES

Daniel Katz (1960) introduced the notion of psychologically dynamic functions of attitudes. He suggested these functions provide a motivational basis for behaviours in terms of predisposing a person either positively or negatively towards situations. In other words, we hold particular attitudes for a particular psychological reason.

(a) **Adjustment function** directs people towards satisfying, favourable and positive rewards and away from dissatisfying and unfavourable punishments. It directs an individual to express an attitude which will be favourably received by society, thus gaining approval such as a reward, and enables an individual to adjust or move away from the expression of an attitude that might be greeted with disapproval (punishment). Politicians might be careful not to espouse racially discriminatory attitudes in case they lose support. An office worker in a mixed gender workplace would not generally state a liking for pornography, as this would probably make colleagues think less of that person.

(b) **Ego-defensive function** protects our self-image from threatening information. Rather than disclose our perceived, or real, failings to ourselves, we adopt an ego-defensive attitude. For example, a person who makes a poor career judgement may adopt an aggressive attitude and defend a 'mistake' by saying he was misled by colleagues.

(c) **Value-expressive function** permits us to express strongly held beliefs and values, which in turn disclose our inner selves to other people. These values or beliefs say a lot about us and what type of person we are. People will often adopt certain attitudes in order to communicate their self-image. For example, people serving voluntarily in famine-hit areas in the developing world are expressing their value system. It is not sufficient for them to sympathise or donate money, they wish to exercise their caring attitude in a more tangible manner.

(d) **Knowledge function**: Attitudes allow us to use our knowledge to attain stability, coherence and consistency in our lives. Our knowledge function guides our feelings and behaviours to ensure, to the best of our ability, neither of these will in any way threaten the likelihood of security, either by displaying inappropriate behaviour (being late) or inappropriate feelings (sarcasm to the boss).

Nutritionists may use their knowledge of diet when formulating an attitude to what they, and others, eat and drink. They may therefore have a negative attitude towards foodstuffs that contain saturated fats, as their knowledge tells them that these have been linked with obesity and coronary heart disease.

5.4 SOURCES OF ATTITUDES

As we know, attitudes are not innate, we learn or acquire them in many ways, from many sources.

(a) **Family**: This is a major influence in an individual's life. Here attitudes are absorbed, almost unconsciously, and are rarely questioned. This is our first experience of interaction with other people, so we learn from it. There is more information on this in Chapter 9 on culture.

(b) **Influential others**: These include reference groups, peers, friends whose opinions we tend to seek out and which are important to us. Their influence on us is quite profound, because we look up to or respect their judgements and we tend to adopt similar views through a need to identify with them. The effect on these influential others on our conformity is also dealt with in Chapter 7 on groups.

(c) **Interaction and direct experience**: We come into contact with situations constantly, causing us at times to re-evaluate our thoughts or views. For example, our attitude towards people with a mental handicap may have originally been fairly negative (i.e. frightened of them), yet through a friendship scheme allowing us to meet and interact with these people, our attitude changes to a more positive frame of mind. Retailers show they are aware of this principle when they give consumers a free test drive with a car or a trial period with a product, to break down preconceptions and to promote familiarity.

(d) **Mass media**: In today's world the media has a profound influence on society. We are directed, cajoled and intimidated into forming attitudes. For example, we saw in section 5.2.1 that some young girls have adopted an attitude towards their body the media have supplied, that to be thin is to be attractive. Obviously there are deeper psychological reasons involved, but the media must claim responsibility for reinforcing the attitude towards a 'perfect' shape.

Similarly, many parents feel that there should be restrictions on the amount and timing of television advertisements for children's toys because of the pressure these adverts place on parents to fulfil their children's wants, especially around Christmas. These parents believe that children are highly impressionable and the powerful medium of television strongly shapes their attitudes.

There are other sources contributing towards attitude function. It is important to remember that there is a dynamic interaction between internal and external forces.

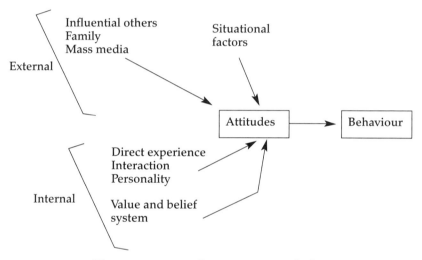

The sources contributing to attitude function.

5.5 TRI-COMPONENT ATTITUDE MODEL

Attitudes are often portrayed as consisting of three major components: cognitive component, affective component and conative component.

(a) **Cognitive component** consists of knowledge and perceptions an individual possesses in relation to the attitudinal object. This component concerns the belief/disbelief element of an attitude. In other words, we use our thought processes to decide whether a manufacturer's claim that their mobile phone is safe is really credible.

(b) **Affective component** consists of the overall evaluation of a person towards the situation. This component refers to the

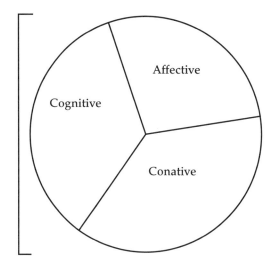

A tri-component attitude model

emotions and feelings element of an attitude. For example, in the absence of scientific data regarding mobile phones causing cancer, would our feelings make us avoid using them and help us form a negative attitude towards them?

(c) **Conative component** refers to the readiness to respond or the likelihood of our response to the attitudinal object. In other words, will we undertake a specific action, such as avoid using a mobile phone if we believe it causes cancer?

5.6 ATTITUDES AND BEHAVIOUR

We have seen the tri-component model of an attitude encompassing the concept of an action component, or a readiness-to-respond component. Next, we must ask how attitudes are linked to behaviour? Some behavioural scientists believe the link between action and attitudes is at best tenuous—an expression of an attitude is not necessarily consistent with behaviour. Others believe there is a very definite connection and that from attitudes we can infer and predict behaviours. At best the link between attitudes and behaviour is interactive, with a number of variables influencing this relationship:

(a) **Intensity:** The stronger and more intense the attitude held, the less it will be compromised, and the more likely it is predictive of behaviour. For example, a person with a strong Catholic attitude to abortion will probably campaign against it being introduced into Ireland.

(b) **Existence of other attitudes:** The existence of a strong attitude may frequently inhibit the behavioural expression of a weaker attitude. For example, an individual may hold that equality is important regardless of class, yet their attitude towards law and order is far stronger. This might mean that they would support tougher policing in high crime areas, even though this may interfere with certain civil rights.

(c) **Ability to respond:** Learning to respond to a particular attitude is often through conditioning. Family, peers and life experience tends to reinforce our long-held attitudes. Therefore if our family has a history of campaigning on social issues, we are more likely to do so as well.

(d) **Situational factors:**

   (i) **Physical environment:** The environment can sometimes inhibit behavioural expression of an attitude, for example it would be rather foolhardy to denounce football hooligans as the source of evil in the world if surrounded by them.

   (ii) **Social environment:** The sensibilities of others often prevent individuals from expressing their true feelings, for example our attitude to animal testing for medical purposes might be somewhat subdued by the presence of 'animal liberators'.

5.7 ATTITUDE MEASUREMENT

5.7.1 Introduction

To understand more fully the concept of attitudes it is necessary to examine the various attitude measurement approaches or scales. It is important to note that all approaches emphasise:

(a) **The direction of the attitude,** whether it is positive or negative, or even indifferent. We might, for example, be against the idea of eating meat, perhaps because of foot and mouth disease.

(b) **The degree** or extent to which the attitude is in that direction. Our view towards meat could be very negative, and we would indicate this by picking the most negative point on the scale we are presented with.

(c) **The intensity of feeling** that goes with the attitude. The level of negativity we feel towards meat may be so strong that we decide to become a permanent vegetarian. This would be measured by open-ended responses in some scales, which would ask about the very negative response which had been indicated.

Scales differ in a number of ways:

(a) **Construction:** The way in which attitudinal measures differ. This may be due to factors such as cost, accessibility to the target population and the nature of the attitudes being examined.

(b) **Response:** Tests differ in how people reply. In some cases they are asked to respond in varying degrees (e.g. a three-point scale would have 'agree', 'no opinion' or 'disagree'), while in other tests respondents are asked dichotomous questions which would be answered by yes or no.

(c) **Dimensions:** With some attitudinal tests it is not so much the person's response on each item but the total score which matters. Respondents are differentiated by total score rather than by the pattern of their responses.

(d) **Scale differentiates amongst people** who are at different points along the scale, placing them in various categories. The nature of these categories depends on the type of scale being used.

The two remaining differences between scales require a more thorough examination.

Firstly, scales are either **manifest** or **latent**. Manifest scales are those that are explicit in the attitude they are testing, with the respondent being aware of the attitude under test, e.g. politics. Latent scales refer to those scales where the subject does not know what attitudes are being examined. For example, the Californian F-scale examines respondents' underlying views towards fascism. This F-scale, rather than explicitly asking the respondent whether they approve of fascism, asks them to what degree they agree with particular statements which do not seem to be overtly connected with fascism, but which test samples have shown to be connected with it. This discloses whether a high probability of displaying fascist tendencies is present or not. This scale could be used by an employer who was concerned about the attitudes of her workforce to the recruitment of a multiracial workforce.

Lastly, the difference between **differential** and **summational** scales. In a differential scale, a subject's responses, are divided into whether they 'agree', 'disagree', or 'don't know'. Summational scales add the scores for each of the responses and come up with a summated, or cumulative, score. Respondents are then compared with reference to the different scores they achieved.

Many of us use summational scales in magazine questionnaires which ask us to rate ourselves on light-hearted items relating to fashion and romance. In these, we are asked to pick which statement applies most closely to our attitudes and then sum the numerical value for each statement to arrive at an overall score, which will indicate which category we fall into.

The following five scales are a mixture of differential and summational scales. The first we shall look at is Osgood's semantic differential scale.

5.7.2 Semantic differential scale

Osgood's semantic differential scale (1957) uses bi-polar adjectives to test attitudes. These adjectives are usually grouped by type: evaluation (good/bad, cold/warm, bright/dull), potency (strong/weak, hard/soft) and activity (active/passive, fast/slow). In all, these particular types of adjectives account for 50 per cent of the concept meaning. In theory, any adjectives can be used, as long as they are bi-polar in nature.

It is a typical seven-point scale, though three or five points may also be used. Some researchers suggest it is better to use a larger set of points because it allows the subtlety of the attitude to be brought out. For example, if testing people's attitudes towards hare coursing, the use of a five- or seven-point scale allows a broader range or scope of answer, for example a response which indicates 'quite cruel', rather than just 'very cruel'. Below is an example of a semantic differential questionnaire on people's attitudes towards the Internet:

Internet Questionnaire

The following are some adjectives that could be used to describe the Internet. Please put a tick beside those adjectives you feel best describe the Internet. Please tick beside all the adjectives.

	+3	+2	+1	0	-1	-2	-3	
Good	❑	❑	❑	❑	❑	❑	❑	Bad
Informative	❑	❑	❑	❑	❑	❑	❑	Confusing
Peaceful	❑	❑	❑	❑	❑	❑	❑	Violent
Interesting	❑	❑	❑	❑	❑	❑	❑	Boring
Cheap	❑	❑	❑	❑	❑	❑	❑	Expensive
Cultured	❑	❑	❑	❑	❑	❑	❑	Pornographic
Observant	❑	❑	❑	❑	❑	❑	❑	Clichéd
Exciting	❑	❑	❑	❑	❑	❑	❑	Mundane
Accessible	❑	❑	❑	❑	❑	❑	❑	Exclusive
Time-saving	❑	❑	❑	❑	❑	❑	❑	Time-wasting

Advantages and disadvantages

Some of the potential difficulties with this scale are the same as those which we will examine in detail later with Likert's scale—that two people may understand different things when given the same adjective. For example, if parents were given the adjective 'violent' in the above questionnaire, some may understand this to mean abusive language, while others may take this to mean actual physical violence. In addition, some parents may not understand the adjectives being given but may be too polite or too embarrassed to say so.

On the positive side, this is an extremely widely used test, is easily constructed, easily understood and, by virtue of being a differential scale, it teases out the subtleties of a person's attitude by examining the pattern of their responses.

5.7.3 Thurstone scale

The Thurstone scale, developed by Thurstone and Chave in 1929, presents the respondent with a limited number of statements (a maximum of between ten and twenty), each with a numerical value. The subject states whether they agree with any of the statements. The total of agreed statements is summed and the researcher has an idea of how the person views the attitudinal object.

The following is an example of the Thurstone scale on attitudes towards the Christian religion.

Scale value	Statement
0.5	I feel Christianity is the greatest agency for the uplift of the world.
2.4	I feel Christianity is trying to adjust itself to the scientific world and deserves support.
5.2	I am neither for nor against Christianity but I do not believe that churchgoing will do anyone any harm.
8.0	I think Christianity is petty, and is easily troubled by matters of little importance.
11.0	I have nothing but contempt for Christianity.

Advantages and disadvantages

Conceived in the early period of psychological research into attitudes, the main disadvantage with this scale is that the initial collation of statements is expensive and designing it is time-consuming and cumbersome, so it tends not to be used much. However, it can be quite accurate.

5.7.4 Likert Scale

Likert developed his scale in 1932. It is perhaps the most widely used attitudinal sampling method in market and social-science research. It presents prospective respondents with statements to which they have to say how much they agree, from 'strongly agree' through 'undecided' to 'strongly disagree'.

There are a number of important points to remember when using this scale:

(a) **The language** of the statement should be simple, clear and direct. The respondent should be left in no doubt as to how to answer the statement, for example 'eating meat is wrong'.

(b) **Simple sentences** should be used instead of compound or complex ones, for example 'The EU has been good for Ireland' rather than 'The EU has benefitted Ireland in every sector since our accession after a constitutional referendum in the early 1970s'.

(c) **Ambiguous statements** should be avoided as this may lead to confusion, for example 'I like the economic policy of the present government'. The ambiguous element here relates to what exactly the economic policy of the government is, and what part of it the person is agreeing with. The question should focus on a particular part of government's economic policies.

(d) **One complete thought** should be contained in each statement. Otherwise, respondents are being asked to respond to more than one question in any one statement, for example 'The EU has not only developed our farming community, but also our road infrastructure'. The difficulty here is that, while you may agree that the EU has helped Irish farmers, you believe that Irish roads are still in a poor condition.

(e) **Avoid statements that may be interpreted as factual,** making some respondents feel they cannot agree or disagree, for example 'The economy is improving.'

(f) **Avoid statements that would be endorsed by everyone.** This particularly applies to statements which wish for goodwill, or aspire to socially acceptable goals, such as 'world hunger should be reduced' or 'I am in favour of world peace.'

If we were testing consumers' attitudes towards a new washing powder product called 'Softclean', a Likert scale might look like this:

Softclean product questionnaire

1. **Softclean cleans clothes without losing softness.**
    Strongly agree ❏ Agree ❏ Undecided ❏ Disagree ❏ Strongly disagree ❏

2. **There's no washing powder as effective as Softclean on the market.**
    Strongly agree ❏ Agree ❏ Undecided ❏ Disagree ❏ Strongly disagree ❏

3. **Softclean is the best washing powder on the market.**
    Strongly agree ❏ Agree ❏ Undecided ❏ Disagree ❏ Strongly disagree ❏

4. **There are no ways in which Softclean could be improved.**
    Strongly agree ❏ Agree ❏ Undecided ❏ Disagree ❏ Strongly disagree ❏

5. **Softclean gets all my stains out.**
    Strongly agree ❏ Agree ❏ Undecided ❏ Disagree ❏ Strongly disagree ❏

Advantages and disadvantages

The disadvantages lie mainly in the danger that statements chosen may be flawed and unrepresentative. Further, it places a great responsibility on the researcher to devise and test appropriate statements. However, the Likert scale is the most commonly used attitudinal scale in market research and in psychology, because it is easy to construct, has a relatively low cost in testing and a straightforward method of data analysis.

5.7.5 Guttman's Scaleogram Analysis

Based essentially on the social distance scale developed by Bogardus (1925), in 1950 Guttman presented his Scalogram Analysis, which placed a strong emphasis on the observation of social attitudes. This scale has been used in social-science and market research. Its idiosyncrasy lies not so much in what it tests but rather in the way that it tests, with its distinctive ordering of statements—the relevance of which we will examine presently. The questionnaire presumes that at the point the consumer responds negatively to one item, that they will also do so to every item after that.

It is a cumulative, or summational, scale to which respondents are asked to answer in a dichotomous manner, either yes or no. It remains a useful tool in examining groupings of social attitudes around a particular attitudinal object.

A typical social distance scale consists of the following types of questions, in the following type of order:

> ❏ I would stand beside a person from another ethnic group at a bus-stop.
> ❏ I would eat in the same restaurant as a person from another ethnic group.
> ❏ I would talk to a person from another ethnic group.
> ❏ I would work with a person from another ethnic group.
> ❏ I would live in the same neighbourhood as a person from another ethnic group.
> ❏ I would live beside a person from another ethnic group.
> ❏ I would have a person from another ethnic group as my best friend.
> ❏ I would happily marry someone from a different culture and race to my own.

We can see from the above that someone who says no to the first statement 'I would stand beside a person from another ethnic group at a bus-stop' is not very likely to say yes to any of the following statements.

This pattern might in turn lead a market researcher to design the following questionnaire to test consumers' views of the technology market.

Market Research Survey

We are interested in your views on products in the technology market. The question we would like you to consider is which of the following items you think are essential for your activities.

Please answer yes or no beside each item:

	Yes	No
MP3 player	❏	❏
DVD player	❏	❏
Mini disc player	❏	❏
Mobile phone	❏	❏
CD player	❏	❏
Video recorder	❏	❏
Television	❏	❏

This questionnaire examines the implicit hierarchy in a consumer's perception of the goods in this area. The goods range from ones which would be quite innovative and purchased by a small section of the population (MP3 player) to others which most everybody owns (a television). How the consumer views the importance of each item will suggest something about the nature of the consumer; are they innovative or are they quite conventional?

Advantages and disadvantages

It is very important in this scale to achieve the correct administration order. Not doing so may lead to inaccuracies in the measurement. To convert various attitudes into potential dichotomous responses can be a complicated and arduous process, as some people interviewed may not respond easily to this dichotomising. As a technique it is laborious, but good for examining small attitude shifts.

5.8 CONSISTENCY MODELS OF ATTITUDES

In this section we examine three of the more popular models of attitudes, which are grouped under the heading consistency models. Put simply, each of these models express a similar premise: that the individual seeks to achieve harmony or consistency in his/her attitudes and behaviour. If tension, upset or inconsistency is perceived, the individual strives to reduce this state of unease to return to a consistent state. We examine three models in this section: balance theory, cognitive dissonance theory and congruity theory.

5.8.1 Balance theory

Put forward by Heider (1946 and 1958), this theory is concerned mainly with dyadic relationships in which one person receives information from another about a particular object. Balance theory states that attitudes towards a person or persons will have positive or negative values, and that there is a tendency for values to change if the system becomes unbalanced, as this causes tension. Rather than suffer tension or inconsistency, the individual will seek consistency by changing an attitude.

For example, if we (A) hold the view that racism (Object C) is wrong and we meet someone (B) whom we like but who believes in racial discrimination, we can either view the person we've met negatively or change our views on racism. In this case, the relationship would be imbalanced. Heider represented this type of relationship in dyadic, or triangular, form with + standing for a positive view of a person or thing and - standing for the opposite.

Balanced and unbalanced relationships can be represented in the following dyadic relationships. Below are examples of each type of relationship:

(a) **Balanced relationship:** Let us presume that we (A) hold a positive view towards someone (B) and that B in turn holds a positive attitude towards a particular object (C), and so do we. The dyadic relationship would look like this:

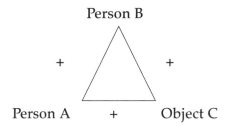

Person B

+   +

Person A   +   Object C

(b) **Unbalanced relationship:** If we suppose that we (A) view a person (B) negatively, that we view a particular object (C) negatively and that B also views the same object negatively, the system is unbalanced. It would appear as:

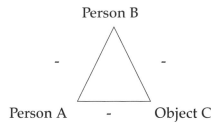

Person B

-         -

Person A   -   Object C

(c) **Another type of unbalanced relationship:** Lastly, if we (A) view a certain person (B) negatively, and we view a particular object (C) positively, as B does, the dyadic relationship would look like this:

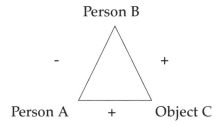

Person B

-         +

Person A   +   Object C

In the last two cases there is a pressure on the individual to change his views on aspects of the attitudes in the dyadic relationship in order to ease the tension and achieve balance. We might change our attitudes about the person or the object, or both.

5.8.2 Cognitive dissonance

Developed by Leon Festinger (1957), the theory of cognitive dissonance describes the cognitive upset or 'mental clashing' that occurs when a person recognises that two thoughts or actions (both held to be true by them) are inconsistent with each other. In other words, they contradict each other. Similar to Heider in his Balance theory, Festinger believes such a conflict results in tension, which in turn motivates the individual to action in an effort to restore harmony or consistency.

Dissonance may be experienced by individuals, when they realise there is inconsistency between an attitude and behaviour. For example, someone may believe smoking is one of the main contributors to lung cancer, yet still smokes. It is important to note that dissonance only occurs if the person *himself* realises the inconsistency in his belief and behaviour. Many of us are able to hold unconsciously contradictory elements in our lives.

Dissonance theory has implications in consumer behaviour. For example, the dissonance a consumer feels is affected by some of the following factors:

(a) The more important the decision the greater the degree of potential dissonance. These decisions are known by marketers as 'high involvement decisions' and usually involve a great deal of emotional or financial input. Buying a house would be an example of this, as it involves a great deal of money, is a decision we make only a small number of times in our lives, and the consequences of a wrong decision are many.

(b) The more alternatives existing, the greater the potential dissonance. So if we are buying a computer the dissonance may be large, as there are many competing brands which often seem similar and cost roughly the same amount.

(c) If there is very little difference between the alternatives, there is much greater chance of dissonance. White goods, such as washing machines and fridge freezers, are goods which tend only to be differentiated by price—if even that. Since they tend to look alike physically as well (where the name 'white goods' comes from) this similarity can also create dissonance in the consumer's mind.

(d) The greater the amount of potentially negative aspects of the goods chosen, the greater the potential dissonance. If we are offered a cut-price round-the-world holiday with an unrecognised tour operator, we may experience dissonance because we want to save money, but we are concerned that the company may be unreliable as they may have little experience in this area. The amount of negatives may be reduced if we go with a well-known travel agent.

The opposite of dissonance is consonance, which Festinger would say we try to achieve where possible. Consumers can achieve this in a number of ways:

(a) The decision can be changed, with the consumer returning the goods or buying the rejected alternative. For this reason, retailers offer consumers money-back guarantees if they are not fully satisfied with the goods after a certain time period, such as 30 days. The consumer feels less pressure, as they know there is a way out if they are not satisfied with the goods.

(b) The consumer can emphasise the positive aspects, and minimise the negative aspects of the goods they have bought. This and the following strategy are also known as 'post-purchase dissonance'. This means that consumers look for information that confirms the correctness of their purchase decision. It is necessary for advertisers to supply consumers with information about the relative superiority of their product because past purchasers of a product, as well as those thinking of buying, are looking for product details.

(c) The consumer can emphasise more the negative aspects of the rejected alternative and reject or ignore its positive aspects.

(d) Attitudes or beliefs can be changed in order to be consistent with behaviour. We might, for example, be against poor pay for manufacturing workers in the developing world, but unknowingly buy a pair of expensive runners from that region. The dissonance we experience when we find out may cause us to change our attitude and maintain that the work benefits the local economy and will give the people a chance to better themselves.

5.8.3 Congruity theory

Developed by Osgood and Tannenbaum (1955), this theory defines consistency as congruity. Osgood and Tannenbaum stipulated that if an individual suffered tension as a result of holding conflicting attitudes or beliefs, something would change in order to re-create a consistency or a return to congruity. An example of both congruity and incongruity is perhaps better explained through the use of the following diagrams:

Congruity

If a football player we admire greatly (giving, say, a +3 on the following scale) endorses and praises a particular pair of boots which we have bought and which we also like (+3 on the scale), there is no discrepancy; both attitudes are at the same point on the scale.

-3	-2	-1	0	+1	+2	+3
						X
						(a) Own boots
						(b) Footballer's endorsement

Incongruity

If a celebrity we like (+2) endorses a product we don't particularly like (-2), the amount of incongruity is equal, i.e. 4. Since there is an equal amount either side the amount of discrepancy will be reduced by equal amounts on either side to 0, as can be seen from the following diagram:

-3	-2	-1	0	+1	+2	+3
	X>>>>>>>>>>>>X<<<<<<<<<<<<<X					
	Object				Person	

Incongruity

If someone we love and trust very much, say a spouse or best friend (+3 on the scale), expresses a negative opinion about a subject on which we hold an opinion (-1), our attitude will change in favour of the more strongly held attitude. In this case, our attitude will change in the direction of the attitude we hold regarding our spouse or best friend. So the less strongly held attitude will probable change from -1 to +2, and our opinion of our spouse or best friend will change from +3 to +2, as we know that they are not an acknowledged expert on the subject. This can be represented diagrammatically as follows:

-3	-2	-1	0	+1	+2	+3
		X>>>>>>>>>>>>>>>>> X<<<<<<<<< X				
	Object					Person

There may be little or no change if:

(a) The person receiving the information does not believe it, her attitude change will not be great.

(b) She only marginally disbelieves what she is presented with, her attitude change will not be great.

In both incongruity examples above, the credibility of the information they are presented with will affect the amount of attitude change that occurs. The consequence of this for marketers and advertisers is (as we will in section 5.10 below on attitude change) that advertising information on their products must be seen as believable.

The final theory of cognitive consistency we will examine is Fishbein's theory of reasoned action

5.9 FISHBEIN'S THEORY OF REASONED ACTION

Fishbein is a theorist who offers a multi-attribute model of attitudes, of particular use in marketing. His treatment of consumer behaviour is far more complex and sophisticated than any of our previous consistency models. Fishbein recognised the interaction between beliefs and information in relation to the attitudinal object and suggested two major models to explain the complexity of consumers' attitudes to particular products.

5.9.1 Fishbein's First Model (1967)

Fishbein put forward his first attitudinal model of reasoned action in 1967. This suggests that an individual's attitude towards an object is a function of the sum of the various composites of that attitude, weighted by the evaluation the person gives to each of the composites of the attitude. In addition, Fishbein believed that people form attitudes towards objects on the basis of their beliefs (perceptions and knowledge) about these objects. Positive or negative feelings are also formed on the basis of the beliefs held about these attributes. His analysis is known as a 'compensating' model, as the evaluations of the various attributes can offset one another.

Fishbein's model is constructed so that a person's overall attitude to some object is derived from their beliefs and feelings about various attributes of the object. This is represented by the following formula, which incorporates the cognitive (belief) and affective (evaluation) components of attitudes:

$$A_o = \sum_{i=1}^{n} b_i e_i$$

where:

A_o =   the attitude towards the object o
b_i =   the strength of belief i about o
e_i =   the evaluation aspects of b
n =   the number of beliefs

An example would be if we were trying to evaluate the attitude of customers to the Internet service provided by Yahoo.com (an Internet service provider, or ISP). Let us say that we were testing four attributes of Yahoo's service: its speed, its information, its comprehensibility, and its cost. The strength or importance of each of these attributes—in relation to the product in question—is determined using a scale going from +3 for high importance to -3 for low importance.

Yahoo.com is costly (b_i):

Likely	_	_	_	_	_	_	_	Unlikely
	(+3)	(+2)	(+1)	(0)	(-1)	(-2)	(-3)	

The same type of question would be used for each of the remaining factors: speed, information, and comprehensibility.

Each attribute can then be evaluated using a scale with +3 being a high evaluation, through to -3 for a low evaluation.

A costly Internet Service Provider is (e_i):

Good	_	_	_	_	_	_	_	Bad
	(Very)	(Moderately)	(Slightly)	(Neither)	(Moderately)	(Fairly)	(Very)	

The scores are summed to give a total attitudinal score; the lower the number the more favourable the attitude. In the case of Yahoo.com the following table could describe the responses of one individual in particular:

Yahoo.com attributes	Importance (b_i)	Evaluation (e_i)	Product $(b_i \times e_i)$
Speed	+3	+3	9
Information	+2	+3	6
Comprehensibility	+1	+1	1
Cost	+2	-1	-2
		Attitude score = 14	

Fishbein attitudinal scale, testing attitudes towards Yahoo.com.

In this case, with four attributes, the maximum score the product could have achieved was 36. As the score is 14, the consumer is giving the product a positive rating, with speed and information being rated the most highly by the consumer.

Advantages and disadvantages

The main advantage of Fishbein's First Model is that it treats attitudes as sophisticated, multidimensional variables, which are weighted and affected by important attributes. The appreciation of the complicated nature of these variables has helped marketers to approach the market in a more informed manner and to emphasise certain aspects of a product in order to improve its marketability.

One of the model's main disadvantages is that a positive attitude does not necessarily mean a consumer will buy the product. In the Yahoo.com example, a consumer may have a very positive attitude towards it after a public demonstration but may not have a phone nor the financial means to subscribe to the service. This discrepancy between a consumer's attitudes towards products and their intention to buy led Fishbein to frame his extended model.

5.9.2 Fishbein's Extended Model (1975)

On the basis of criticisms of his first model, Fishbein reviewed his model and proposed his extended model with the help of Azjen (Fishbein and Azjen, 1975). This states that a person's intention to act towards a product (for example, their purchasing behaviour) is a function of how she perceives the item, what consequence the act of buying may lead to and the chance she thinks the good has of achieving that consequence. In other words, the difference between the scales that would measure these variables and the ones used for Fishbein's earlier attitude model is that focus is now on the consequences of purchase behaviour rather than the attributes of the object. This produces a function that describes the chance of an individual performing the act of buying a product.

The following formula represents this idea:

$$A\text{-act} = \sum_{i=1}^{n} b_i e_i$$

where:
A-act = the individual's perception towards performing a particular act (e.g. subscribing to Yahoo.com)
b_i = the individual's perceived belief that performing the behaviour will lead to some consequence i
e_i = the individual's evaluation of consequence i
n = the number of salient consequences involved

The product is then quantified in a manner like that used for the first model, of reasoned action. In the example of Yahoo.com below, the consumer is asked to rate from +3 (high belief that using Yahoo.com will lead to the perceived consequence) to -3 (low belief). They are then asked to rate, from +3 (high evaluation) to -3 (low evaluation), their evaluation of this consequence.

Consequences (Yahoo.com)	Perceived belief (b_i)	Evaluation (e_i)	Product $(b_i \times e_i)$
Wealth	+1	+3	+3
Efficiency	+2	+3	+6
Innovation	+1	+1	+1
Time-saving	+3	+2	+6
		Attitude score = 16	

The consumer who filled out the above believed that Yahoo.com would most likely lead to saving time and this was a consequence he rated quite highly (i.e. +2). Conversely, the interviewee believed that using Yahoo.com would be less likely to lead to wealth (+1) and innovation (+1)- though these were consequences they rated highly (+3 for both).

All things considered, Yahoo.com scored slightly higher using this model (16 out of a possible 36) as on the model of reasoned action (14 out of a possible 36). To enhance this perception further, Yahoo.com would need to advertise possible consequences of using the product, and how desirable these are to the group being targetted. For business people, this would include cost savings, efficiency and reliability and a study which suggested that Yahoo.com could deliver these desired consequences.

Loudon and Della Bitta (1993) have represented this concept in the following diagram:

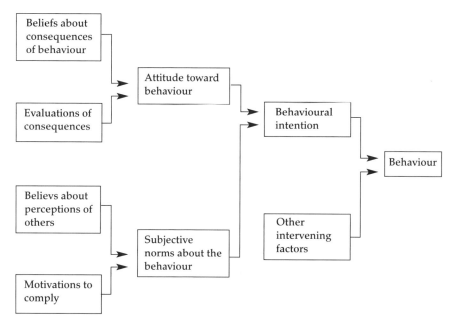

A diagram of Fishbein's Extended Model.

Criticisms

The main criticism of this extended model is that it still does not predict whether a consumer will actually buy a particular product on the basis of their attitude, though it does give us a better picture of what they think of the particular product—especially because it examines not just how the consumer views a particular product, but also how she views the act of buying the product.

5.10 ATTITUDE CHANGE

In previous sections we have noted how long-lasting and persistent attitudes are. The likelihood of changing a person's attitude is quite slim, given that—according to Katz (1960)—each attitude provides a function. He believed it was impossible to change an attitude, until we first realised the function it served for the individual concerned.

It can be difficult to change attitudes, and a useful method available to politicians, marketers and others wishing to implement a change is through communication.

A simple model of the **communication process** shows this point.

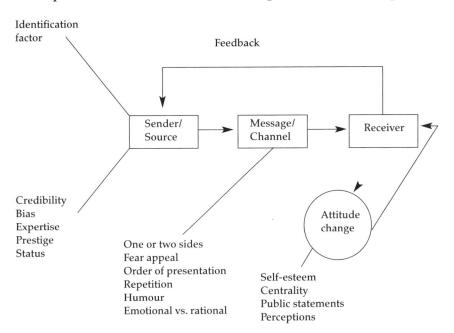

5.10.1 Source factors

Many factors influence the process of attitude change within the sender variable, whether the sender is a company, group or an individual. We review several of the major factors:

(a) **Credibility:** The higher the credibility (perceived by the receiver) the sender or source possesses, the greater the likelihood an attitude will change. When advertising basketball clothing and equipment Michael Jordan has a lot of credibility, as he is one of the best basketball players in the history of the game.

(b) **Bias:** If the sender is perceived as being in any way biased towards their message, the receiver's orientation towards the sender decreases, leading to little, if any, attitude change. Michael Jordan also advertises sunglasses, but we might feel that he is biased about the product if we knew that the reason he does this is that he owns part of the company that produces them.

(c) **Like or identify with receiver:** If the sender is liked or can be identified in any way with, and by, the receiver, attitude change may occur. Physical characteristics such as gender, age and attractiveness can influence the receiver's attitude. Boy and girl bands are often used by soft-drink and confectionery producers to advertise their products because the main consumers of these tend also to be fans of these bands. This is similar to the concept of 'reference groups', which we will examine in Chapter 7 on groups.

(d) **Perceived expertise:** If the communicator is perceived as being expert or as possessing high qualifications to speak on the topic, influence may occur. Advertisers use Olympic medal winners to endorse their goods, as the general public perceive these sportspeople as having expertise.

(e) **Prestige/Status:** More credibility is attached to a communicator if they are perceived to have status or prestige through either occupation, wealth or title. Often, prestige and status are attributes given to individuals by society. Certain professionals, such as accountants or doctors, are respected for their expertise. This may have an effect on our behaviour, even when these professionals are trying to change our attitude about issues other than those in which they are most qualified: financial and medical services.

5.10.2 Message factors

If the communication process is viewed as a completely interactive process, it is important to understand message factors.

(a) **One/ two sides of message:** In general terms, presenting one side of the message is effective if the audience is already in agreement with the communicator. The message serves to reinforce views or beliefs. By presenting two sides of a message, there is an impression that the message is being handled fairly and objectively. This is more effective if the audience is undecided.

However, opinion tends to be divided in this issue. Recently, the issue has centred on the educational level of the audience. If educated, they are regarded as being more perceptive and will welcome the opportunity to decide for themselves by being presented with a two-sided message. Those who are less well educated are said to appreciate the simplicity of a one-sided argument or message. Producers may refer to the concern of consumers but may cite 'independent research' to justify their claims. They will often place great store by a comparison between their product and competing ones that ranks their product highest.

(b) **Order of presentation:** Where should the relevant and important parts of a message be placed in order to have the most impact? A general rule of thumb would be:

  (i) **Beginning of the message:** If there is a low level of audience interest, the marketer might mention price reductions at the start of the message to capture the consumer's interest.

  (ii) **End of a message:** If there is a high level of audience interest, such as for the Minister of Finance when he is delivering the budget speech, the most important part of the message (adjustment of tax levels) will be delivered near the end.

(c) **Primacy and recency effect:** In two-sided messages, is it better to present important parts of the communicator's stance first (primacy) or last (recency)? Again, opinions differ, but generally the last part heard tends to be the best remembered. This is why advertisers will pay more for their products to be positioned at the end of an ad break so that it will be the last to be perceived.

(d) **Reasons/Conclusions**: To maximise audience favour, it is important the message addresses a number of issues:

(i) Why they should listen.

(ii) Use of questions to generate involvement.

(iii) Use of concrete items rather than abstract terminology.

(iv) Use of familiar examples.

(v) Draw conclusions for audience.

Producers will often use these points in sponsored programmes—typically for car valeting and kitchen/cooking equipment—where they can control the amount and type of information disseminated.

(e) **Fear/Humour appeals:** The use of message appeals is extremely important. Fear appeal centres on avoidance of social disapproval (for example, use this deodorant if you don't want to be ostracised) and physical danger (decrease your alcohol intake to avoid drink driving).

Humour appeal should be used selectively, as it may lose its effect after a relatively small number of exposures. Generally, when humour is used in a message it aids retention of the message and concentrates the audience's mind on less serious issues. It tends to be used to differentiate between quite similar, or very new, products rather than for high involvement (important) product choices, such as a mortgage.

5.10.3 Receiver factors

Here we concentrate on the audience, or receiver, variables and how these affect the communication process.

(a) **Personality**: Generally, the more confident and the higher the self-esteem of the receiver, the less persuadable or in need of social approval they are. In other words, attitude change may not occur for this type of receiver as their attitudes to life are well thought out. This is not necessarily related to age. However, young children, especially what marketers now call 'tweenagers' (between eight and 12 years of age), are very susceptible to television advertising.

(b) **Centrality:** The importance or the centrality of the attitude held by the receiver will denote whether change will occur. For example, the more central the attitude is to a receiver's value system, the less likely the attitude will be changed. Irrespective of any nutritional value an advertiser may emphasise, observant Jews and Muslims are unlikely to buy non-kosher and non-halal meat, which their religions does not allow them to eat.

(c) **Public statements:** If the receiver has publicly stated an attitude towards a particular topic or object, this act alone will more than likely prevent attitude change. This has been the basis for certain retailers issuing so-called 'loyalty' cards, which encourage consumers to continue shopping in certain outlets once they have publicly stated their preference.

(d) **Functions of attitudes:** As we noted earlier, whatever function or motivational base a particular attitude serves for the receiver, no matter how persuasive the communicator is, the receiver will not change his attitude unless the alternative provides a similar function, that it is ego-defensive, value-expressive. Consumers buy products from The Body Shop because they believe that doing so expresses their concern for the environment and for animal rights. A manufacturer bringing out an innovative hair-care product—which might satisfy the ego-defensive function—will not succeed in changing these consumers' minds unless it can also claim not to have harmed animals in the product testing—the value-expressive function.

Whether we are a marketer, an organisational manager or a member of the general public, an understanding of the functions and basis of attitudes is essential. In many cases, attitudes are well thought out, strongly held and resistant to change. Even with a forceful attitude change, message we must thoroughly investigate the source, strength and complexity of these attitudes. We hope this has given you an idea of the issues involved.

5.11 SUMMARY

1. Attitudes are learned predispositions to act in a favourable or unfavourable way to an object or situation.

2. Attitudes fulfil four motivational bases or functions: adjustive, ego-defensive, value-expressive and knowledge.

3. We learn attitudes from a great variety of sources: family, peers, friends, culture, media and experience.

4. An attitude consists of three components: cognitive, affective and conative.

5. Attitudes and behaviour are linked but depend on a variety of interacting factors.

6. There are four principal scales for measuring attitudes: Likert, semantic differential, Guttman and Thurstone.

7. Consistency theories of attitudes (balance, congruity and cognitive dissonance) state an individual will always act to regain mental consistency if disharmony exists.

8. Fishbein's Theory of Reasoned Action offers a more complex and sophisticated attitudinal model depicting the interaction of beliefs, values and knowledge bases.

9. Attitude change is difficult to achieve. The communication process, using sender, message and receiver variables, offers opportunities to attempt attitude change.

5.12 EXAM QUESTIONS

1. You are a marketing professional and you have been asked to change the attitudes of the general public towards an Irish political party. Suggest ways, using the methods of attitude change, you could bring this about. (Institute of Technology, Tallaght, 2001)

2. Examine the consistency theories of attitudes.
   (Institute of Technology, Tallaght, 1997)

3. Describe in detail Fishbein's proposals on the measurement and structure of attitudes? (MII, 1998).

4. Evaluate the ways in which attitudes may be measured. (MII, 1997).

5. What are the functions of attitudes?

Chapter 6

Personality

I am three men: the person I think I am;
the person other people think I am,
and the person I really am.

Mark Twain (1835-1910)

6

Personality

Learning objectives

After studying this chapter, you should be able to:

1. *Present an informed and comprehensive opinion about the nature of personality.*

2. *Explain the basic aspects of Sigmund Freud's psychoanalytic theory of the mind.*

3. *Identify Jung's psychological types within personality development.*

4. *Describe Cattell's trait-based personality theory.*

5. *Understand Carl Roger's 'nurturing' approach to personality.*

6.1 INTRODUCTION

Personality is a multidimensional concept. Most people use the term 'personality' in a descriptive way, as in 'she has a warm, friendly personality'. Psychologically speaking, this is incorrect. Behavioural scientists speak of personality in broader terms, stressing the interaction of a number of processes, such as attitudes, motives and values. Despite all the years of research on the topic, no one agreed definition has emerged.

Scientists broadly agree however on one fact, personality should be viewed in terms of the **totality** of a person's functioning, rather than focussing only on specific attributes. Another perspective, called situationism, states that we must look at the situation, as it will determine the expression of our personality. This approach suggests that the most important aspect for us is the context, rather than a personality that exists irrespective of where we are and who we are with.

A knowledge of personality theories provides us with a basic understanding of a person's orientation, whether towards a product (consumers), an employer (work attitude), or towards social issues. This chapter begins with the questions posed by researchers so that we will see the parameters used for a definition of personality. Next, two orientations of study are introduced, the notion that personality is inherent and fixed and the contrary one that it develops and changes.

Lastly, we examine four important personality theorists: Freud, Jung, Cattell and Rogers.

6.2 DEFINITION OF PERSONALITY

Despite the large number of differing theories, researchers have found common ground in the questions that should be asked when approaching an understanding of personality. For example:

(a) What is personality made up of?

(b) What variables go into making up personality, and are they permanent or transient?

(c) Is our personality already formed when we are born (nature) or are we completely shaped by the environment (nurture). Is it a mixture of both?

(d) How can one accurately measure, by means of tests, a person's personality?

(e) How accurate are these tests?

(f) How much of a person's personality is shown to the outside world?

(g) To what extent can we ever know our own personality?

(h) Is our behaviour unique or is personality common to all of us as human beings?

The theories in this chapter address these questions in varying ways. Each presents a different perspective on, and definition of, personality. Even though some of the following theories may differ, the definition of personality we propose is from Gross (1992):

> Those relatively stable and enduring aspects of individuals which distinguish them from other people, making them unique, but which at the same time permit a comparison between individuals.

6.2.1 Nomothetic and idiographic approaches to personality

The main difference between approaches to personality research lies in whether personality comprises permanent traits or characteristics or whether personality involves studying unique individuals, or variables, so as to arrive at an overall understanding of personality in general.

Raymond Cattell favours the first category. He believes our personalities are composed of factors that are relatively permanent universal traits. These factors last through our lifetime and can be measured and analysed by means of psychometric tests. According to Cattell, the interpretation of personality is made more accurate by identifying and measuring relevant traits. This is known as the **nomothetic** approach.

The second main approach, the **idiographic**, states that because we are unique; we display personality characteristics reflecting our own idiosyncratic characters. This view is shared by psychoanalytic theorists, such as Freud and Jung, and humanistic psychologists, such as Maslow and Rogers. These theorists suggest that rather than analysing individual traits and trying to 'add together' a personality, we must look at the complete expression of a personality in a person's behaviour. Further, they would say someone's personality can change by means of psychoanalysis, the intervention of other professionals, as well as through self-reflection.

6.3 THEORIES AND THEORISTS

6.3.1 Sigmund Freud

Sigmund Freud is perhaps the most famous psychologist/psychiatrist/psychoanalyst to have contributed to an under-standing of the human mind. He was the first of the major theorists on personality.

Sigmund Freud (1856-1939)

For someone who wrote so extensively and has been so widely translated, he is also one of the most misunderstood writers in the field of psychology. How often do we say that someone has committed a Freudian slip—saying what we really mean by accident—without having been formally introduced to this term and without really understanding what it means? Many of Freud's phrases and ideas have come into common usage without being fully understood and without being put in context properly.

Regarding context and criticisms, it should be borne in mind that Freud was a writer of his time, a writer concerned primarily with sexually repressed patients in Vienna in the late nineteenth and early twentieth century. We may take it for granted today that each of us has a subconscious mind. Such a fact was unknown when Freud began his work as a psychiatrist.

Outside the clinical sphere, Freud's ideas are used by some in marketing to segment the market for particular products, and this segmentation is called psychographics. We will give examples of how his ideas are used in organisations and in marketing after explaining each of the main aspects of the theory.

Structure of personality

Personality, according to Freud, is the result of psychic energy. This energy finds expression through three strong, interacting mental forces: the **id**, the **ego** and the **superego**.

Put simply, our personalities are formed by the interactive nature of these three forces, constantly vying for psychic energy in order to fulfil their purposes.

The id

The id is the deepest and strongest source of psychic energy. It works solely on the 'pleasure principle' of immediate and total satisfaction of its needs, regardless of the consequences. It exists to avoid discomfort and pain and to experience only pleasure. It operates on a subjective and subconscious level, tending not to recognise objective reality or to realise that some desires are socially unacceptable, such as aggressiveness.

Application: Marketers of food products such as chocolates use this principle by saying 'go on, treat yourself', to ignore the consequences and do something which brings you enjoyment. Some workers display this principle when they are persistently late; they have not developed the ability to moderate their own desires to achieve a compromise with those with whom they work.

The ego

Working on the 'reality principle', the ego deals with the outside world, attempting to control the id by channelling psychic energy into socially acceptable and realistic behaviours. The ego—in dealing with the actual—acts as a mediator of psychic energy, helping individuals deal realistically with their environment.

Application: Since the ego seeks to 'balance' the competing demands of the id and the superego, food producers can achieve this by suggesting a certain chocolate brand is low in fat. This will satisfy the desire for chocolate (an id impulse) and the desire to abstain from anything fattening (a superego impulse).

A worker who was involved in an ego orientation would recognise—using the above example of lateness—that he might wish to stay in bed (an id impulse), feel guilty at this prospect (a superego impulse), yet realise that he will be able to sleep in when not working (an ego impulse).

The superego

Working on the 'moral principle', the superego is regarded as the conscience of the individual. It comprises the conscience (the actions which our parents or guardians believe to be wrong, punish us for committing and about which we feel guilty) and the ego ideal (the actions which our parents or guardians encourage us to perform, reward us for performing and which make us feel proud). It attempts to control the id's basic instincts (which are frequently socially unacceptable), while influencing the ego in terms of moral rather than realistic actions. The superego strives for the ideal. The superego is only in part conscious, which may be explained by how we may feel guilty over an action that our reason says is not immoral.

Application: When presented with advertising for food which is fattening or unhealthy we may reject it (a superego impulse). To counteract this, advertisers need to emphasise the nutritional aspects of a product, including chocolate!

A worker who was engaged in a superego orientation would be very concerned about complying with all the rules and regulations of the organisation. She would be unlikely to be persistently late. If she were, she would suffer guilt.

A simple example of the three forces at work is: the id demands chocolate now (pleasure), the superego (conscience) tells us dinner is ready and not to spoil our appetite, while the ego (reality) suggests we have the chocolate as dessert.

The following diagram (from Dworetzky, 1985) shows how the id, ego and superego integrate structure of the conscious and subconscious mind, according to Freud.

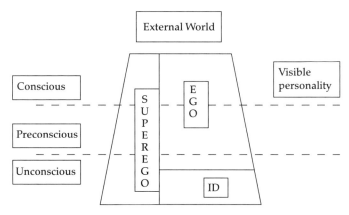

The types of consciousness outlined above may be understood as follows:

> According to Freud, at any given moment some of our thoughts and information are in the **conscious**, others are in the preconscious and still others are in the unconscious. The conscious consists of whatever thoughts are currently the focus of attention, whereas the **preconscious** consists of stored thoughts and information which could be retrieved and brought into consciousness without much difficulty. Finally, the **unconscious** consists of thoughts which are very difficult or impossible to bring into consciousness. For example, traumatic childhood experiences are often located in the unconscious mind. (Eysenck, 1998)

Stages of development

Personality is defined by the interactiveness of id, ego, superego and how they handle psychic energy or tension. How our personality develops, according to Freud, is through a psycho-sexual process, consisting of five stages. The presence of the id, ego and superego is with us constantly throughout our developmental stages, but really begins operating when we reach maturity. A young infant, for example, tends to be all 'id', demanding constant satisfaction, while a child of eight to ten years begins to enter the 'age of reason' and of moral considerations (superego).

The psycho-sexual developmental process consists of five stages, each possessing physical importance for the infant or child. Progress through each stage is of utmost importance in terms of adult behaviour in later years. Freud pointed out that we do not necessarily pass peacefully through these stages, nor is there a rigid time structure. Those who fail or become stuck (for which Freud used the term 'fixate' to be dealt with below) in any one stage tend to exhibit behavioural problems in adulthood.

Freud defined the main developmental stages as:

Stage	Age	Characteristics	Adult behavioural problems
1. Oral	0-1	Concerned with senses, of which mouth is the most sensitive. Can turn out to be orally incorporating or orally expulsive.	e.g. silent or chatterbox.
2. Anal	1-2	Concerned with controlling its defecation. May turn out to be anally retentive or anally or expulsive.	e.g. tight-fisted or very very generous.
3. Phallic	2-5	Has to cope with resolving its Oedipus or Electra complex, and may learn to identify with same-sex parent.	e.g. confused sexual Orientation.
4. Latency	5-12	Sexual thoughts or behaviour are put into the subconscious. Also, superego and id go into subconscious.	e.g. inability to take part in ordinary life.
5. Genital	12 on	In this stage the person reaches mature adult sexuality.	

(a) **Oral stage:** The child is concerned exclusively with its physical senses, the mouth being the most sensitive. This can carry over into later life with an adult being either orally incorporating (they try and acquire knowledge or collect things) or orally expulsive (they become very sarcastic or argumentative in later life).

In a marketing context, marketers may seek to satisfy the needs of oral incorporaters by trying to sell them goods which appeal to their desire for knowledge, such as educational courses, books or even encyclopaedias. The needs of orally-expulsive consumers may be satisfied by commercial radio phone-ins or particular types of video programmes.

(b) **Anal stage:** The child—through its parents and toilet training—learns to control its defecation. In complying with its parents' wishes, the child progresses normally through this stage. Alternatively, the child can either be anally retentive or anally expulsive. In either case, the child may do so to displease its parents or to establish its own independence. In anal retentiveness, the child may turn out to be excessively stubborn or concerned with detail, order or cleanliness.

A marketer could appeal to this type of person by emphasising products that promote cleanliness and order, such as detergents and filing systems. In the case of anal expulsiveness, the child may develop into an adult who is disorderly, destructive or cruel. Marketers may target them as the type of individuals who prefer products emphasising individuality and nonconformity.

(c) **Phallic and latency stages:** The child is highly concerned with its genitals. The Oedipus complex (for a male child) and the Electra complex (for a female child) exists here. These are mechanisms by which the child learns to resolve (in most cases) its feelings of sexual attraction towards its parent of the opposite sex, ultimately identifying with the parent of the same sex.

Between the end of this stage and the beginning of the final stage, there is the latency period (between the ages of 5 and 12) where feelings and actions already described are put into the subconscious at the age of 5, to re-appear at the age of 12. The difference is that, at the age of 12, the adolescent is developing sexual feelings and a concern for others in his/her environment, whereas previously he/she was self-centred.

Marketers frequently target this stage by emphasising sex-role stereotypes to adolescents, teenagers or even adults who wish to identify with the fashion and behavioural habits of their own sex. The converse can also be true, and marketers may wish to target those who are not satisfied with the fashion norms that currently exist.

(d) **Genital stage:** Through this the child reaches mature adult sexuality. Marketers would target people who see themselves as sensible, mature adults wanting to live up to the responsibilities of life.

Defence mechanisms

The peaceful channelling of psychic energy by the three personality components (id, ego and superego) is more often than not achieved. However, there are occasions when the ego (reality principle) fails as a mediator, causing tremendous psychic tension, which in turn results in an unresolved situation. Rather than suffer this tension, the individual devises defence mechanisms. These are unconsciously determined techniques brought into existence to deal with the state of tension. A great number exist, and we highlight several here:

Fixation: In an effort to avoid new situations, with their concomitant challenges and insecurities, individuals cling to what is familiar. Individuals fixate in what to them is a familiar, tried-and-tested routine, for example instead of progressing to a more challenging and responsible role, an employee may remain over-qualified in his/her present job.

Projection: To eliminate anxiety or tension-filled emotions from our own minds, we project such states onto others because we cannot handle them, for example we project feelings of insecurity onto others rather than express them ourselves.

Repression: Purposeful forgetting of threatening information in order to cope with the present situation, such as denying the existence of upsetting knowledge.

Regression: To regress or return to behaviours more suitable to earlier stages of development, because of an inability to cope with the present situation, such as tantrums.

Although Freud's theory has had profound effects on later psychological theorists, such as Adler and Klein, a number of criticisms have been levelled at his work:

(a)   It is a very sexually orientated theory with the notions of self-concept and self-esteem scarcely examined.

(b)   Freud's theory is deterministic in the sense that it paid little heed to external factors; it was for him a process begun at birth and continued regardless of experiences. Personality, for Freud, was largely determined by the age of five.

(c)   The theory dismisses cultural or societal influences and so is a personality theory regardless of societal norms, values and institutions. Freud held that all personalities develop in this particular way, without social or cultural influence.

(d)   He dismisses individual differences, such as attitudes, motives, and the ability to empathise.

(e)   The theory is potentially unscientific. His research consisted of case studies and interviews, with quantitative measurement omitted and data not given.

These are the main aspects of Freud's theories. For a fuller exposition of his work, we recommend the references given at the end of this book.

The next theorist, Carl Gustav Jung (1875–1961), at one stage a colleague of Freud's, was also a proponent of the psychoanalytic view of personality.

6.3.2 Carl Gustav Jung

Jung's conception of personality is of a dynamic psyche, self-regulating and in constant movement with energy flowing between two opposing poles. When energy flows to the progression pole, the individual is concerned with active adaptation to his/her environment, while regression energy manifests itself in the satisfying of unconscious needs.

In this idea of opposites in personality development, Jung focussed on the concept of people constantly trying to adapt to their own, and society's, needs. He placed great emphasis on cultural and spiritual contributions to personality development, noting that the inner or psychic process is equal in value to the environmental or outer process.

Jung also believed that everyone has not only a personal unconscious (containing individually repressed or controlled memories and impulses), but also a collective unconscious, a kind of memory bank in which are stored all the images and ideas the human race has accumulated since its evolution from lower forms of life.

The collective unconscious of people in countries in the EU would be very different as their cultures are quite varied. Further, the relative sizes and levels of importance of the countries would also affect each nation's collective unconscious.

The collective unconscious in Ireland is greatly affected by the fact that for many years the country tried to establish its independence from England. This has led to some saying that Irish people like gaining a victory, in business or even in sport, over much bigger and more important rivals.

Some of the images in the collective unconscious are called archetypes, because they consist of classic images or concepts. The idea of mother, for instance, has become an archetype, as everyone is born with a kind of predisposition to see and react to certain people as mother figures. Other archetypes are of the 'wise old man', 'the dashing young maiden' and 'the brave young warrior.' As these images apply so widely across cultures, they are frequently used in advertising, for example they are used extensively by soft-drinks manufacturers running global campaigns.

Jung's theory of personality manifests itself in the notion of psychological types, that the flow of energy results in either outward orientation or inward orientation—again the opposites. Instead of identifying specific stages in personality development, Jung stated that there are eight basic personality types: four main types, each with two sub-divisions into introversion and extroversion. The first two functions Jung categorised as rational (thinking and feeling) and the last two as non-rational (sensing and intuiting).

Jung suggested that people come to display differing degrees of introversion (a tendency to focus on our inner world) or extraversion (a tendency to focus on the social world) and differing tendencies to rely on specific psychological functions, such as thinking (intellectual), feeling (evaluative), sensing (senses) and intuiting (intuitive).

The functions of Jung's personality theory

Function	Introversion	Extraversion
Thinking (intellectual)	Rationally analyse consequence of situations for themselves.	Rationally analyse consequence of situations on others.
Feeling (evaluative)	More likely to have reflective and self-conscious feelings.	Emotions are more likely to include others.
Sensing (senses)	Those who are aware of the world around but whose activities are more inwardly directed.	Sensitive to the outside world but directed towards others in their activities.
Intuiting (intuitive)	Subconscious understanding of the world, directed inwards.	Subconscious understanding of the world, directed towards others

(a) **Thinking function** (our intellectual function): 'Thinking' people react to situations analytically and are very conscious of the implications of their actions for themselves and for others. Jung believed there were both introverted and extroverted thinking types. The difference was that introverted types were more likely to direct mental energies towards their own activities, whereas extroverted types were more likely to direct their energies towards interaction with others. An example of an introverted thinking type might be a reclusive university professor, and an extraverted thinking type, an outgoing, enthusiastic teacher.

In marketing, financial packages would appeal to this type of person, as they would rationally evaluate all the competing facts and figures. The introvert/extravert dichotomy would determine whether it was for themselves (introvert and the financial package mentioned above) or directed towards others (extravert, as in the case of someone who campaigns for the environment).

(b) **Feeling function** (our evaluative function, by which we accept or reject things on the basis of positive or negative impulses): 'Feeling' people react to situations with emotions such as friendliness, joy or even suspicion. Introverted feeling types are more likely to have reflective, self-conscious feelings (like certain types of journalists who try to capture the mood of the moment). Extraverted types are more likely to embrace others and direct their energies/feelings outwards (for example cheerleaders). A marketing executive should present these people with images of emotion, either in terms of themselves or of others.

(c) **Sensing function** (our sense function—smell, touch, taste, sight—about the world around us): This might be termed the artistic function as it includes those who are highly aware of the world around us. Simple examples of the introverted and extroverted sensing types might be, respectively, a novelist or a poet (who have to withdraw from the world by the very nature of their work) and an actor or street performer (who are usually very outgoing, expressive types).

Marketers, in appealing to the sensing individual should use evocative imagery (such as colourful pictures and distinctive sounds) or stimuli (such as such as stirring music). Some advertisers also use 'smell strips' in magazines, so that consumers can try a sample of a particular fragrance.

(d) **Intuiting function** (our subconscious perception of our world, by which we may have a hunch about something): Intuitive people use empathy as a basis for communication, for example in the way a psychologist might seek to understand a patient. Once again, the introverted types direct this understanding towards themselves (such as someone who uses fortune tellers to gain an insight into their future). Extroverted types direct it towards other people (such as those involved in caring professions). This type of person may be interested in self-help products (introverts) or in charities (extraverts).

Sometimes, Jung believed, our personalities develop as a function of interaction with our physical, mental and cultural environments. Although he stipulated his eight personality types, he recognised that they were not mutually exclusive. We can see from the above that some of the professions mentioned could have people from any one of the eight different personality types.

In conclusion we can say the following about Jung's personality theory:

(a) Jung provided a valuable contribution to the study of personality, as he sought not just to explain it in terms of Freud's idea of predominant sexual energy, but rather in terms of fuller concepts such as the society and culture in which we live.

(b) Jung based his research on a greater number of people and cultures throughout the world than did Freud whose research was largely based in nineteenth and early twentieth century Vienna.

(c) Jung's idea of a collective unconscious is a powerful idea of mental functioning which helps in understanding the similarities between cultures and races that may have little or no contact.

(d) Jung's personality types are very useful in the analysis of different types of people. They have also been used in marketing, in segmenting markets according to personality type.

(e) As in the case of Freud, Jung's theory is potentially unscientific. His research consisted of case studies and interviews, with quantitative measurement omitted and data not given.

6.3.3 Raymond Cattell

Cattell did not place emphasis on the structure of the conscious and subconscious mind. Instead, he sought to understand personality by analysing what he believed were the roots of our personalities, what he called traits. He defined a trait as 'an inferred mental structure that accounts for the consistency of observed behaviours'. He divided traits into two categories: **surface** and **source** traits.

The understanding of these two types of traits is central to an understanding of Cattell's theory of personality. Simply stated, Cattell believed that our personality is a function of the interaction, or balance, between these two types of traits.

Surface traits are ones that are usually readily apparent in a particular individual, for example Mary is vivacious, friendly and generally outgoing. **Source traits** are harder to discern. Cattell stated that source traits are combinations of parts of a person's make-up that are not readily apparent and emerge only when we subject these personality constituents to close mathematical analysis. According to Cattell, source traits (the deeper traits) interact with each other to produce surface traits, which in turn leads to a particular expression of personality.

The importance of source traits was highlighted by Cattell when he introduced a further sub-categorisation system: **constitutional** and **environmental** mould.

(a) **Constitutional source traits** we are born with and they remain the same throughout our lives.

(b) **Environmental mould source traits** are dynamic (goal-oriented), responding to changes within our environment and are also further divided, determining how well goals are achieved.

   These are subdivided into:

   (i) **Ability traits** which determine the effectiveness of an individual's efforts to achieve a particular goal.

   (ii) **Temperament traits** which are how, at what speed and at what energy level an individual attempts a goal.

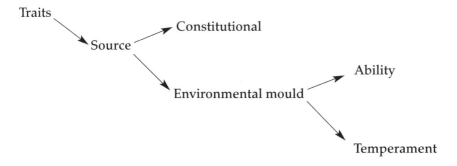

Cattell's categories of personality traits

The structure of Cattell's personality theory

Cattell attempted to ground his theory of personality structure in a realistic manner. He devised the 16PF (or personality factors) personality questionnaire, which attempts to measure personality. The 16PF consisted of the traits Cattell felt made up an individual's personality.

Letter symbols and personality factor (PF) names		
Outgoing	A (Affectia–Sizia)	Reserved
More intelligent	B (Intelligence)	Less intelligent
Stable	C (Ego strength)	Emotional
Assertive	E (Dominance–Submissiveness)	Humble
Happy-go-lucky	F (Surgency–Desurgency)	Sober
Conscientious	G (Superego strength)	Expedient
Bold	H (Parmia–Threctia)	Shy
Tender-minded	I (Premsia–Harria)	Tough-minded
Suspicious	L (Protension–Alaxia)	Trusting
Imaginative	M (Autia–Praxernia)	Practical
Shrewd	N (Shrewdness–Artlessness)	Forthright
Apprehensive	O (Guilt proneness–Assurance)	Placid
Experimenting	Q1 (Radicalism–Conservatism)	Traditional
Self-sufficient	Q2 (Self-sufficiency–Group adherence)	Group-tied
Controlled	Q3 (High self-concept–Low integration)	Casual
Tense	Q4 (Ergic tension)	Relaxed

Cattell used mathematical techniques in personality research. His 16PF is analysed through factor analysis: a mathematical procedure devised to tease out which source and surface traits are inherent in the questionnaire respondent.

It is important to note that Cattell tackles the issues in the 'nature and nurture' debate in that he believes we are born with traits that stay with us throughout our lives (constitutional source traits), but also possess traits that which develop and change in response to the conditions around us (environmental mould source traits). He states it is the constitutional source traits that are predominant in the forming of personality.

Cattell's theories have been used a great deal in the business world. The 16PF is a very versatile tool in personnel selection, as it can easily categorise individuals into different types and determine whether they are suitable for the job in question.

Uses for the 16PF have also been found in the educational and marketing fields, yet there are criticisms of his theories. For example, his structuring of personality theory is within the confines of mathematical techniques and so could be said not to pick up the subtleties and irrationalities of human behaviour. His approach to theorising attempts scientific methodology, but pays little heed to the concept of the unconscious, or the idea of the self.

Nevertheless, his work attempts to clarify the theory of personality in clear unambiguous terms introducing the coherence and precision of an empirical approach.

6.3.4 Carl Rogers

A proponent of the humanistic or self-concept development of personality, Carl Rogers' theory of personality was developed from his clinical experience in his famous 'person-centred psychotherapy'. Rogers (1902–1989) holds the view that people are naturally orientated towards positive actions and growth. His work with patients highlighted two constructs, or components, of personality:

(a) **Organism:** The physical and psychological functioning of the individual, incorporating the totality of conscious and unconscious experiences. Rogers said that the organism includes the **phenomenal field** (which includes the totality of conscious and unconscious experiences) and the self. Rogers said that the individual's phenomenal field 'can never be known to another except through empathic inference and then can never be perfectly known'.

(b) **Self-concept:** The self of the self-concept comprises the 'I' of an individual's own perceptions and characteristics, and the 'me' in relation to others. Embedded in this component is the notion of an ideal self (what we strive to or would like to achieve) and the actual self (the actual me, as I now perceive I am).

In personality development, Rogers believes both components are affected by our experiences, and our relationships with others. If we experience what he referred to as 'unconditional acceptance'—the acceptance of ourselves as we are by our parents and important others, rather than the placing of conditions of love based on the extent to which we achieve their goals—throughout our lives, we will feel secure in ourselves. Personality development for Rogers is a process where the organism and the self are in harmony. Problems arise when this unconditional acceptance is transformed into 'conditional acceptance', and individuals experience **incongruency** or **denial**.

Incongruency manifests itself in an upset between the organism and the self, between what we are and unrealistic or unfair expectations of how we should be. According to Rogers, a healing can take place if true acceptance is given and the individual feels secure.

Rogers' theories are used by managers who set realistic goals (ideal self) for their staff whose abilities they know (actual self). If unrealistic goals are set, the staff will probably not achieve them and they may feel that the manager regards them less highly, and so they may believe themselves to be less valued. Therefore, managers must create a work atmosphere where workers are valued for their ability and potential, rather than using 'one size fits all' management techniques that can be implemented—often unsuccessfully—irrespective of whom the manager is managing. They must also encourage workers to view themselves accurately—and not pessimistically—so that they can see if they are close to achieving their ideal self. Rogers conceived of happiness based on the individual being able to realistically evaluate and attain congruency between their own self and their ideal self.

This theory has promoted the idea of the 'self' in personality theory, bringing recognition within scientific circles of the therapeutic process. To bring clarity to a complex topic, Rogers has attempted measurement through self-reports, interviews and group work. His theory does not emphasise the unconscious element within personality development and is often regarded as too optimistic and simplistic in that, according to Rogers, it is possible to heal and make whole all people instead of concentrating solely on personality disorders. The psychoanalytic theorists disagree with this contention.

The four very different approaches to personality development have shown us that personality is a complex concept. We examined whether it is expressed through behaviour; whether it is expressed through internal feelings and emotions; whether it consists of traits, or whether it is moulded through the environment and experience. Does the unconscious play as a big a part as Freud would have us believe, or is it as clear-cut as Cattell suggests? Whatever approach or orientation is adopted, it is important to realise that no one theorist provides the answer. Personality consists of many facets. Our knowledge of personality theory can only offer *suggestions* as to why people behave as they do.

6.4 SUMMARY

1. Personality is difficult to define but generally consists of relatively stable and enduring aspects.

2. Freud suggests personality is made up of three components: the id, the ego and the superego, developed in five stages.

3. Jung places more emphasis on the cultural and social development of personality and says it is expressed through four personality types (thinking, feeling, sensing and intuiting), each of which has two sub-categories (introverted and extraverted).

4. Cattell believes personality is comprised of surface and source traits whose interaction produces a personality type. He invented the 16PF test, a questionnaire attempting personality measurement.

5. Rogers states that personality is a developmental process between the self and the organism, believing that positive and unconditional acceptance leads to an optimistic and happy personality.

6.5 EXAM QUESTIONS

1. Explain Rogers' theory of personality. Describe the ways in which it could be used in the work of an accountant. (Institute of Technology, Tallaght, 2001)

2. Contrast the theories of Freud and Cattell. (MII, 1998)

3. Compare and contrast Freud's and Jung's personality theories.

4. Show how nomothetic theories of personality differ from idiographic theories by describing one example of each type of theory. (MII, 1996)

5. 'Where Cattell is explicit and precise, Freud is implicit and unclear.' Discuss.

Chapter 7

Groups

Many of the quests for status symbols—the hot automobile, the best table in a restaurant or a private chat with the boss—are shadowy reprises of infant anxieties ... The larger office, the corner space, the extra window are the teddy bears and tricycles of adult office life.

Willard Gaylin (1984)

7

Groups

Learning objectives

After studying this chapter, you should be able to:

1. *Understand what is meant by a group and some of the reasons why people join groups.*

2. *Explain the different categories of groups.*

3. *Identify the nature of group structure, its processes and stages of development.*

4. *Discuss how groups exert power over members' behaviour.*

5. *Describe the Hawthorne Studies.*

7.1 INTRODUCTION

Studying individuals together in a group, one would expect to be relatively simple—as it is a collection of individuals. This assumption is incorrect. Once individuals begin interacting and interrelating with each other, a subtle and pervasive force is at hand. Hackman and Morris (1975) suggest, that while '... something important happens in group interaction ... there is little agreement about what that "something" is.'

Our lives are made up of many groups: family, peers, social and work, to name but a few. Each has rules and influences our behaviour. In this chapter we examine many group issues: why and how they develop, why people join, what types of groups exist. Perhaps one of the most important questions addressed is why groups are so influential?

From an organisational viewpoint, management may wish to harness what is referred to as synergy, the collective output of a group stimulated by member interaction. Work groups are mostly created by management to perform particular tasks or functions. But they sometimes emerge naturally as a consequence of the division of labour. Managers must be aware that understanding and managing group dynamics is an important part of their role.

An example of a group with a strong identity

From a marketing viewpoint, the concept of group formation and membership has tremendous implications. Work and social groups influence consumer-related attitudes and activities. Frequently, consumers are unaware that they look to others for direction as to which products to buy. Indeed, these others are also unaware that they serve as a consumption-related model, or reference group as it is called.

In everyday life, group membership influences social involvement. Being a member of a particular group can fulfil many psychological needs, such as security, esteem or just companionship. Knowledge of group dynamics offers insight into our own and others' behaviour.

We begin by defining a group and discussing the varied reasons people have for joining. We next examine the various categories along with the structure and development of groups. Lastly, we address the question of the power of a group and how it may influence individual behaviour.

7.2 GROUPS

7.2.1 What is a group?

Furnham (1997) defines a group as more than two people who 'communicate regularly, share goals and interact with each other over time, so building up affective (or emotional) bonds' (p. 429).

A group can be seen as any number of people who:

(a) Interact with each other.

(b) Are psychologically aware of each other.

(c) Perceive themselves to be a group.

In other words, they have a collective identity, a sense of being related as a result of interaction with each other. All three of the above conditions must be met for a collection of people to call themselves a group.

Frequently, a cinema queue or bus queue is referred to as a group, purely because they happen to be in close proximity. This is psychologically incorrect. Such a collection of people is merely an aggregate of people. Traditionally, the idea of physical proximity was thought to be a necessary component for group definition. With the advent of advanced communications technology, people may only meet in a 'virtual' sense and yet still have strong affective ties to each other.

It is important to understand that the behaviour of individuals both affects and is affected by the group: a two-way relationship exists.

7.2.2 Reasons for joining a group

People have many different reasons for joining groups. We join to fulfil a need (or needs). By joining one group, several needs can be served at one time. In general, we join for the following reasons:

(a) **Security:** We feel secure if we belong to a group. The maxim 'safety in numbers' highlights this fact. Whether facing a new situation or a new challenge, being part of a group reduces anxiety. Take, for example, joining a social club. It would be normal to feel awkward and embarrassed, experiencing that 'everyone knows everyone else' feeling. If on the other hand we join on a new members' night, we immediately feel less anxious because we are one of the crowd. We feel secure because of the 'protection' offered by the group.

(b) **Affiliation:** The need for companionship or the presence of other people centres on this affiliation need. Often, a group is a source of personal value to an individual because it satisfies the need for being in the company of others.

(c) **Social identity:** People see themselves as psychologically intertwined with a group, that is, the group can often reflect our self-image. Groups, as diverse as Young Mums and Toddlers groups and Vincent de Paul, help us to establish a sense of identity with like-minded people. The group 'grounds' us, providing both security and a sense of self. We feel we belong. Work, interest and friendship groups all offer a sense of identity.

Being part of a group can make people feel secure and support their sense of identity.

(d) **Goals:** When an individual recognises the mutuality of her own goals with a particular group's goals, she frequently responds by joining. The group's power is often greater than the individual's, so it makes sense for them to join forces. Where this is the case, the individual tends to be prepared to offer both commitment and time. Take, for example, the Neighbourhood Watch Scheme, which plays an integral role in residential areas. Individual and group goals are similar—to prevent crime— but how much more powerful is the combined effort?

(e) **Activities:** We sometimes join a group because its activities offer us satisfaction. In sports clubs, for example, many members wish only the enjoyment of playing the sport or keeping fit. In the same way, people join night classes because they wish to participate in the activity and not necessarily to become experts.

(f) **Inter-personal attraction:** This may be the most obvious of reasons for joining a group—because of the attractiveness of its members. There are three influencing factors:

(i)   Perceived ability of the group.

(ii) Perceived status of the group.

(iii) Similarity in attitudes, beliefs and values.

There are other reasons for joining groups, such as proximity, physical attractiveness, race and economic self-interest. It is important to note that whatever our reasons (often unconscious), we seek fulfilment within the group structure. In return, there is a trade-off: we must adapt within the group. This is one of the most important aspects of group psychology examined later in the chapter.

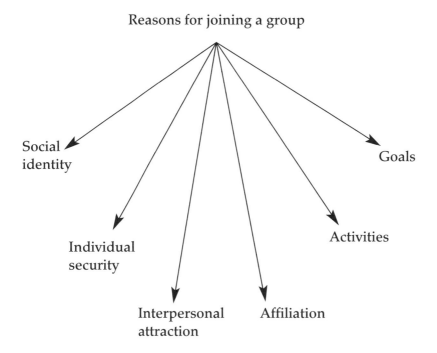

7.3 CATEGORISING GROUPS

It would be almost impossible to function in society without belonging to a group. They exist everywhere: family, friends, work, socially. It is not until we stop and think about it, that we realise just how many groups we belong to and influence in our lives. Groups tend to differ in purpose and size and it is this difference that enables us to categorise or classify them.

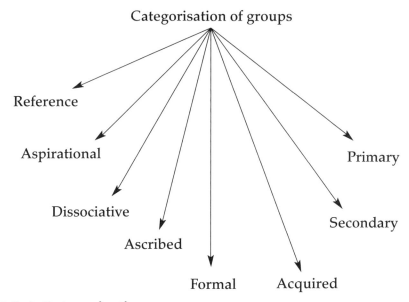

7.3.1 Categorisations

In general, the following categorisations exist:

(a) **Ascribed groups**: Membership is not voluntary, we have no choice in the matter, for example family, school class, nationalities.

(b) **Acquired groups**: Membership is voluntary, we actively seek to belong, e.g. sports, social clubs.

(c) **Primary groups**: Small, intimate group with member communication and interaction on a one-to-one basis, such as a study group, a family or a marketing team.

(d) **Secondary groups**: Large group with less continuous interaction than in a primary group, but group identity is sufficiently present. The main distinction between primary and secondary groups is the importance and frequency of interaction, for example a head office is a secondary group to a regional office.

(e) **Formal groups**: Consciously created by management to meet the needs of the organisation with a clear group structure, well-defined tasks and predetermined working procedures. Formal groups are characterised by a high management involvement in all aspects of group activities, such as a special task force, a committee or a government body.

(f) **Informal groups:** Established by its members, it is socially active and consists of friendship or interest groups. Management must recognise the importance of informal group structure because frequently these groups exercise strong control over their members, e.g. social groups of friends.

(g) **Aspirational group:** An individual's perception of a group causes them to want or aspire to join, for a variety of reasons, such as perceived status. Aspirational groups can have a profound influence on non-members' behaviour because of their strong desire to join the group, for example a local yacht or golf club.

(h) **Disassociative group:** This works in reverse to the above group and has a negative influence. Individuals avoid being identified with such groups, for example drug takers, joyriders.

We can be members of any number of such groups, adapting relatively easily to their respective rules and regulations. There is, however, one more important categorisation we must examine, that of the reference group.

7.3.2 Reference group

A reference group or groups are those an individual uses, or refers to, in determining her judgements, beliefs and behaviour. Our first reference group is the family, from which we adopt values, judgements and attitudes. Other reference groups follow: school friends, peers, work associates. In fact, any of the above group categorisations may act as a reference group.

Reference groups often determine an individual' behaviour, in the sense that they:

(a) **Provide comparisons:** Individuals attempt to match and emulate reference group behaviour.

(b) **Provide guidelines:** Individuals perceive and adopt rules that govern members' behaviour.

The concept of a reference group is used widely in marketing. It is generally acknowledged that consumers accept reference-group influence because of the perceived benefits in doing so, such as status and identity (Loudon and Della Bitta, 1993).

With so many categorisations, are all groups structured in the same way? Is there a difference in make-up between say, an informal group and a reference group? Group structure may differ in cohesiveness (strength of group bonds) or status (power levels), but it always refers to the way its members relate to each other.

7.4 GROUP STRUCTURE

Group structure may be defined in terms of a relatively stable pattern of relationships among particular aspects of a group. These aspects, or differentiated elements, consist of cohesiveness, status, roles, norms, communication and size. We examine these in order to understand how each contributes towards a picture of a group.

7.4.1 Cohesiveness

This refers to the motivation of members to remain in the group. It encourages conformity, stability and sharing activities. Group cohesiveness results from 'forces acting on the members to remain in the group' (Festinger, 1950) and includes:

(a) **Interaction of members**: The more frequently people meet, the more they get to know each other and the more they perceive themselves as a group. This in turn eases communication among members and fosters group identity.

(b) **Goals and tasks**: If tasks and objectives are clear, unambiguous and relevant, members will feel a greater sense of motivation and achievement.

(c) **Mature development of group**: The longer the group has been in existence, the more likely members are prepared to continue their association with, and participation in it.

(d) **Homogeneity**: The more similar members are in areas such as attitudes, motivations, education, status, the more they will share common perspectives and group goals.

(e) **Nature of external environment**: If individuals perceive their environment as hostile, a group offering protection will be welcomed and loyalty and commitment given.

7.4.2 Status

This refers to the assigning of a power level to an individual, such as the chair or the treasurer. The assigning of status within a group serves three important functions:

(a) **Motivational**: Status provides reward/incentive basis for performance or achievement, for example an employee may be encouraged to perform particularly well if a promotion such as head buyer is on offer.

(b) **Identification**: Status provides useful cues for acceptable behaviour towards hierarchical relationships. It is useful in a job to know the chain of authority because most of us tend to alter and/or adapt our behaviour towards work colleagues according to the position they hold.

(c) **Stability: Status** provides continuity in areas such as:

    (i) **Authority patterns**: Provides a steadying influence by knowing where authority lies.

    (ii) **Role relationships**: We know how to act and respond to various colleagues.

    (iii) **Interpersonal relationships**: We get to know and respond to people in their particular roles.

These three functions provide individuals with a consistent and unambiguous knowledge of group hierarchy. A question often asked is 'Is there status in informal social groups?' The answer is yes. Despite a lack of a definite structure or goal-directed behaviour in informal groups, leaders still emerge (see 7.6.4 below) and a rather more subtle status hierarchy operates. For example, status may take the form of wealth, occupation or popularity. A group, whether formal or informal, still has a hierarchy.

7.4.3 Roles

This refers to the part an individual plays or adopts in a group. A role is basically a self-contained pattern of behaviour. Each role, whether leader or back up, has its own pattern of behavioural expectations imposed by society. A mother may perceive her role as nurturing, encouraging and sympathetic. A supervisor may perceive her role as motivational, administrative and organisational. Whatever the role, an individual perceives and enacts role expectations with varying degrees of success.

Within organisational life, roles may be divided into three general areas:

(a) **Task**: Where the role concentrates on task-related activities, ensuring the group achieves its goals and maintains its schedule, for example the role occupied by the chairperson of a meeting.

(b) **Relations**: Where the role focusses on social relationships within the group to promote:

(i)   Harmony.

(ii) Welfare.

(iii) Cohesiveness.

This role attempts to promote a positive, rewarding atmosphere concerned more with members' feelings than with the task in hand, for example personnel officer or counsellor in a company.

(c) **Self-orientation**: This role emphasises the specific needs or goals of an individual, frequently at the expense of the group. It is often referred to as a group member having a 'hidden agenda'. In other words, the member possesses ulterior motives and does not fully participate within the group work ethos, for example where a businessperson uses a voluntary group to enhance her company's performance.

Within the context of defining roles, two further points are important:

(a) **Role ambiguity**: This refers to the uncertainty of an individual as to:

(i)   The exact nature of the job or role they have to perform.

(ii) Others' expectations of the same role.

This can cause stress, insecurity and loss of self-confidence. It is extremely important that role requirements are explicit and unambiguously stated, making it easier for individuals to conform.

(b) **Role conflict**: This occurs when expectations about an individual's role in the group contradict each other:

(i) **Inter-role** conflict occurs when an individual experiences conflict between two or more roles, such as the difficulties in trying to be both a boss and a friend to a work colleague.

(ii) **Intra-role conflict** occurs when an individual receives contradictory messages concerning the same role, for example the difficulties for shop assistants when the boss marks the limit of their authority, yet customers often challenge assistants to take more responsibility.

How an individual perceives and carries out his role in the group has important implications for its overall functioning.

7.4.4 Norms

This refers to a standard against which the appropriateness of behaviour is measured. Two norms in our society are that we go about fully clothed and we use knives and forks to eat our food. In other words, a norm is the expected behaviour in a certain setting.

Group norms develop for the following reasons:

(a) They provide an agenda for acceptable/unacceptable behaviour.

(b) They provide roles for members in order to reduce confusion or ambiguity.

(c) They provide for group survival. If deviant behaviour threatens the smooth flow of performance, the group will isolate or reject such deviance.

(d) They provide identification for members.

Pressures to conform to group norms are powerful determinants of group behaviour. In short, norms act as regulatory mechanisms. As these emerge, individuals begin to behave according to how they feel other group members expect them to behave. The acceptance of norms by a group member facilitates integration into the group and is taken as a signal that the individual concerned is committed to the group.

An academic study of the emergence of a group norm was carried out in Muzafer Sherif's Auto-Kinetic Effect experiment (Sherif and

Sherif, 1969). He demonstrated how three individuals' different opinions converged as they gave repeated public estimates (over a four-day period) of the apparent movement of a point of light within a darkened room. The auto-kinetic effect creates a perceptual illusion in which a light that gives the appearance of movement is in fact stationary.

Individuals' opinions differed widely on Day 1 of the experiment. Day 2 and Day 3 saw a moving closer together of opinions. Sherif postulated that this was because they heard each other's public statement and began to doubt their own perceptions and began to agree with their fellows because of covert pressure. Day 4 saw a total convergence; the group of three had established a group norm, and felt satisfied they had seen the same thing.

The phenomenon of the moving statue at Ballinspittle, Cork, may be a real-life example of Sherif's study. A story began that a statue of the Virgin Mary had begun to move. The (mostly white-painted) statue was in a dark grotto at some height above eye level. As crowds gathered to observe this phenomenon, a consensus emerged that the statue was indeed moving. Miracle or combination of perceptual illusion and group convergence? You decide.

7.4.5 Communication

This refers to the process of information being given in order to initiate/complete goal behaviours. There are two general modes of communication within groups:

(a) **Centralised**: Information is channelled through one person with other group members having little or no interaction. Progress or regression on tasks is the responsibility of one person.

(b) **Decentralised**: Information is free-flowing; group members are at liberty to cross lines of authority to accomplish goals.

The task in hand tends to dictate the communication mode. Where tasks are functional, centralisation is favoured. The more creative the task, the more likely that communication is decentralised. For example, jobs that are basically straightforward can be standardised with one-directional communication. Jobs demanding creativity require a free flow of information and communication, so ideas and messages can be shared and discussed.

7.4.6 Size

This refers to the number of group members. Group size can have an important effect not only on performance but also on interaction. Generally, the smaller the group the more frequent the communication and interaction between members. Goal accomplishment tends to be reached very quickly with more member accountability. Small groups are usually less formal than larger groups and possess an ease of functioning.

Larger groups, however, tend to have a higher generation of ideas, use of more resources and a larger expertise/skill base. It is true that there may be a more formalised communication pattern, which in turn may inhibit participation, but company/group objectives can be more structured and goal accomplishment more easily attained.

7.5 GROUP DEVELOPMENT

7.5.1 How groups develop

The more individuals share in activities, the more they interact. This in turn leads to a discovery of shared perspectives and often shared goals. These are the seeds of group development.

Groups are not static entities; like individuals, they are dynamic and constantly changing. It is generally accepted that all groups develop over a five-stage period. Depending on members, task and resources, these stages vary in time scale. It is important to note that not all groups pass peacefully through these five stages. Some groups disintegrate within the first or second stages, leaving tasks incomplete and people dissatisfied. If groups do happen to re-form, they must return to the first stage and start the development process all over again.

7.5.2 Stages of group development

Tuckman (1965) proposed a five-stage model of how groups develop. This was later developed by Tuckman and Jenson (1977). It is one of several conceptual models existing in the area of group dynamics. Tuckman's model is fairly simplistic but reflects quite accurately how people assume a group identity and begin to operate as one. The stages include: forming, storming, norming, performing and adjourning.

Forming

Members meet, usually for the first time, and attempt to find themselves a place in the group. It is a process of testing out the new environment.

(a) **Feeling**: Members experience anxiety and uncertainty in a new environment. They attempt to share feelings and risk, disclosing personal information about themselves.

(b) **Task**: Members are unsure of how to go about their task, schedule or agenda. They find it difficult to evaluate one another's suggestions because they are unfamiliar with the task and each other.

(c) **Social**: Members search for a sense of personal identity in the new group and tend to rely on others for guidelines. Previous experience is discussed, but sensitive issues are not yet broached.

(d) **Leader**: Authority is rarely questioned in this first phase. Members, unsure of themselves or their position tend to accept and rely on guidelines already set out.

Storming

Members experience conflict in areas such as goals, norms or status. They clash over adoption of roles and much effort is made, through overt means, to clarify group tasks.

(a) **Feeling**: Members are vying for identity. They begin to question decisions, disagreeing with one another. For some, this stage is a challenge; for others, conflict inhibits.

(b) **Task**: Members openly express differences in opinions and task expectations.

(c) **Social**: Members feel more secure on a personal level and make more self-assertive statements or actions. The group has not yet 'jelled', or become clearly defined, and social relationships are still being tested. Norms and attitudes are in their early stages.

(d) **Leader**: Members, becoming more assertive, feel free to question decisions made and the leader is frequently challenged.

Norming

The group is beginning to experience an identity. Members become more accepting and group success, rather than individual success, provides a sense of unity and purpose.

(a) **Feeling**: Members have begun to accept each other; tolerance rather than conflict is the overriding feeling. Individuals feel much more secure within the group and begin to experience satisfaction and cohesion.

(b) **Task**: There is more open and reasonable discussion in this stage, members recognising the need for co-operation and goodwill. Tasks and roles are assigned and accepted.

(c) **Social**: Members adapt to the group structure. Harmonious interaction is at its peak with co-operation in every sphere.

(d) **Leader**: The leader is no longer challenged but accepted and trusted with the task of organising goal accomplishment. The leader is frequently helped by group members, who accept delegation of tasks for the good of the group.

Performing

The group's overriding aim is goal accomplishment.

(a) **Feeling**: Members experience unity of purpose, satisfaction and motivation.

(b) **Task**: Members unite in striving for task accomplishment. Creativity and evaluation are often encouraged.

(c) **Social**: Members experience mutual support and encouragement. Bonds of friendship are formed. Attitudes become more clearly defined and norms are accepted and obeyed.

(d) **Leader**: Similar to previous stage.

Adjourning

This is the final stage during which tasks are completed and group relationships begin to disengage. Some groups have clear points of disbandment, such as a project team with a task deadline. Others find the point for ending their activities more ambiguous and occasionally problematic, as some team members move on and others linger on.

A group evolving through all five stages will develop into an effective and productive entity. Members will be co-operative and motivated with tasks being accomplished on satisfying terms. As noted earlier, groups that fail to proceed at their own pace through these stages will not develop completely, nor will they be productive.

Interestingly, once a specific task is completed, the group, on commencement of a new task, tends to retrace its steps through the same five stages. If group membership remains the same, then stages 1 (forming) and 2 (storming) are passed through relatively quickly in order to re-experience the group cohesiveness and productivity exemplified in stages 3 (norming) and 4 (performing).

Although the five developmental stages occur in all groups, they are not as distinct as we have portrayed them. However, depending on the size and type of membership, it is often possible to identify a particular stage. This may be advantageous in a work situation where management, aware of group-development dynamics, recognises understands and responds to the groups at its various levels of development.

Once a group has assumed an identity, having worked through the first four stages, it becomes a very powerful factor.

7.6 GROUP POWER

7.6.1 Power

The power of a group lies in its ability to control its members and ensure they possess a shared frame of reference; that is, a shared view of a particular situation. This shared frame of reference not only aids goal accomplishment, but also ensures group survival. It has been suggested the recent successes of the British Labour Party are in no small measure due to their rebranding as 'New Labour' and the degree to which all party members are kept 'on message', that is, put forward shared views on every political issue.

What happens when the group's power is questioned? Any deviations from the norms or any challenges are regarded as a threat. The group responds by closing ranks and imposing certain (usually agreed) sanctions such as fines or disbarment. Why do people 'obey' the group, or allow it so much power?

7.6.2 Reasons for conforming

People obey the group rather than risk exclusion. This conforming behaviour occurs for a number of reasons:

(a) **Fear of rejection:** If a person has worked hard to become a member of a group for whatever reason, they tend to accept roles and norms imposed by the group rather than suffer rejection.

(b) **Unanimity among members:** It is difficult to be a minority of one and to resist the pressures of a group of individuals. Psychological research indicates that when a group's unanimity is broken, so also is its social power. (Morris & Miller, 1975).

(c) **Perceived attractiveness:** If a group is perceived as attractive, desirable or possessing status, it is more than likely its rules will be accepted. (Mullen, 1985).

(d) **Gains to be made:** If an individual perceives gains are to be made by remaining in the group, a trade-off will occur. The individual will accept group rules in return for gains.

(e) **Ambiguity of stimuli:** The greater the number of ways stimuli may be interpreted, the greater the likelihood of conformity by the group. In other words, where there is no one correct and obvious interpretation of a situation, individuals tend to reach group agreement. See Asch's 1956 experiment on page 180.

(f) **Degree of self-esteem/personality variables:** It has been suggested (Hall & Lindzay, 1985) that there are connections between conforming behaviour and personality traits. Individuals requiring social approval tend to be more conforming in their behaviour.

7.6.3 Research into conformity

If we draw together the strands of this chapter, we begin to understand how powerful groups are in encouraging conforming behaviour. Conformity may be defined as 'a change in behaviour or belief … as a result of real or imagined group pressure' (Kiesler and Kiesler, 1969). It is the behavioural result of being affected by how others act as well as acting as others do.

The following two pieces of research highlight the conforming nature of individuals.

Asch's Line Experiment (1956)

Social psychologist Soloman Asch believed in the concept of conformity, yet expressed reservations as to whether, when an unambiguous stimulus was presented, conforming behaviour would follow.

His experiment consisted of seven subjects (one naive and six confederates) and a series of trials depicting lines of various lengths. Confederates is the name used in psychology for individuals participating in an experiment who are instructed to act in a particular way by the experimentor. 'Naïve' refers to subjects unaware the experimenter is manipulating their confederates. The task in this experiment was to match Line X with a line of similar length, i.e. A, B or C.

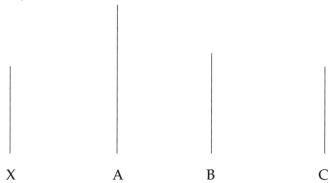

The six confederates or helpers were:

(a)   Unknown to the naive subject.

(b)   Instructed to make incorrect judgements on previously selected trials; that is, they deliberately chose the wrong lines as previously agreed with Asch.

The naive subject was placed second to last and so witnessed five other volunteers' opinions, before being asked to give his/her own. In over a third of the trials, the naive subject agreed with the confederates in what were obviously incorrect selections. According to Asch, the naive subject denied his/her own senses, preferring to agree with the others and follow the norm set.

Milgram's Study of Obedience (1974)

Stanley Milgram's controversial experiment examined conformity to authority. Asch's (1956) and Sherif and Sherif's (1969) research highlighted covert group pressure to conform, where no clear pressure was put on individuals to conform. Milgram presented his conforming behaviour experiment to see how far people would respond to overt pressure from a figure of authority.

Milgram's experiment consisted of:

(a) Confederates ⎫
                   ⎬ matched one to one
(b) Volunteers   ⎭

(c) Electric-shock generator assessing the intensity level, moderate through to fatal.

The experiment was presented to volunteers as the effects of punishment on learning abilities. A volunteer had to teach a confederate a series of word pairs. When errors were made in recall, the volunteer was instructed to administer an electric shock. The more errors made, the stronger the intensity of the shock.

At this stage, it is important to make several points clear:

(a) Milgram's aim was to see if ordinary individuals would obey the authority figure and knowingly give various electric shocks to other people.

(b) The confederates were work colleagues of Milgram and NOT connected to any electrical apparatus, but were told to scream when 'punished'.

(c) Volunteers truly believed they were administering waves of electrical currents to another individual (witnessed by the fact that volunteers sweated profusely, became agitated and visibly upset).

(d) Each pair (one volunteer and one confederate) were seated either side of a screen, visual eye contact was blocked.

When Milgram described his intended experiments to a group of 110 psychiatrists, college students and middle-class adults, they responded in this way:

(a) Self-estimates of electric-shock intensity would not exceed 135 volts (between moderate and strong); that is, if in a similar situation, they would not administer very heavy electrical currents.

(b) Others might reach the intense level (300 volts); that is, other people might go further (self-bias perception coming into play).

(c) No one expected the fatal dose to be administered.

(d) Psychiatrists suggested that the likelihood of (c) being reached, would be one in a thousand, with that individual being seriously mentally disturbed.

The actual results of the experiment were highly unexpected with 63 per cent of volunteers reaching 450 volts (a fatal intensity), despite hearing supposedly agonised screams from behind the screen. Needless to say, Milgram's experiment was denounced as unethical; the imposition of mental or physical abuse in the name of psychological research is strictly forbidden. Nevertheless, it did point out that well over half his volunteers conformed to authority to the extent that they were willing to administer fatal electrical shocks.

7.6.4 Hawthorne Studies

No work on groups would be complete without mention of the Hawthorne Studies. Carried out by Elton Mayo in the 1920s in the Western Electric plant, Chicago, USA, these studies were among the most extensive and influential in any area of social research.

Mayo, a member of the National Academy of Sciences, was invited to research the Theory of Effects of Altered Illumination on work procedures within the Hawthorne plant. Put simply, the idea was that the better the light, the higher the productivity.

A two-group experimental design was carried out with surprising results. Rather than only one group increasing their work rate (the group receiving brighter illumination), both groups' work rate increased. After repeated experiments with similar results, Mayo concluded that it was not the altered illumination that increased productivity but the fact that the workers concerned in the experiments were receiving extra attention from management.

The so-called 'Hawthorne Effect' is that extra attention given to individuals increases their sense of importance, which in turn enhances performance. We can see the Hawthorne Effect operate in everyday life; children as well as adults feel and perform better when acknowledged or when positive attention is paid to them.

Mayo stayed with Western Electric for a number of years to advance his research and became interested in group theory; how effective groups are in a working environment. Mayo initiated a series of studies during the 1920s and 1930s observing and interviewing shop-floor workers at the Hawthorne plant. The three main phases of his work involved the relay assembly room studies, an interview program and the bank wiring room experiments.

Relay room

This study involved six female workers, who were allowed to choose their own group of work colleagues and were observed over a period during which work rates, rest periods and finishing times were continuously altered. The aim was to establish under which condition the women worked hardest. In fact, the women's productivity rate increased regardless of whether conditions were altered positively or negatively. The following conclusions were drawn:

(a)   The Hawthorne Effect came into operation; the women's sense of importance increased because they felt they were helping the company to solve problems. The conditions set out by management, such as work rates, were not influencing factors.

(b)   The women felt a sense of belonging, stability and purpose in being part of their group. These factors resulted in good relationships between women and supervisors, low absenteeism, higher motivation and record levels of production.

The interviews

Mayo carried out over ten thousand interviews at the Hawthorne plant. The interviews focussed on levels and causes of worker satisfaction. Not surprisingly elements like poor physical working conditions were associated with expressed dissatisfaction. Mayo also felt that many of the responses to the interviews were based on sentiment rather than rationality. He interpreted such responses as indicating that levels of work satisfaction may have more to do with the social organisation of work rather than factors in the immediate work situation. To investigate these ideas further he carried out a series of studies in the plant's bank wiring room.

The bank wiring room

This involved male workers being observed by a neutral observer who concluded that:

(a) Natural leaders, who were not necessarily those appointed by management, emerged within the group.

(b) Codes of conduct, such as norms and rules, originated from and were practised by the group.

(c) The group instigated its own authority regulations without management having to supervise.

(d) Deviants from the group were punished by the group.

See Huczynski and Buchanan (2001) for detailed observations on the Hawthorne Studies. Ours is an overview of Mayo's work from which the following conclusions may be drawn:

(a) Informal groups will always form in work situations and possess a recognised structure.

(b) Work is essentially a group activity.

(c) Groups fulfil the needs for belonging, stability and security present in most people.

(d) Natural leaders emerge from groups.

(e) A worker is a person who tends to be conditioned by the social demands of the work group.

(f) The informal work group is capable of exerting tremendous pressure on individuals to conform to group norms.

(g) Deviants are punished or isolated if the group is threatened.

The importance of Mayo's research lies in the fact that it marked the beginning of the age of modern management theory. Mayo conceived workers as not purely motivated by money but also sensitive to personal attention from management and co-workers. He felt that employees worked more productively and positively when a group atmosphere prevailed. Theorists such as Vroom and Adams further supported Mayo's conclusions.

The presence of groups in our lives is pervasive. We do not and cannot exist in isolation. Any one of us is a member of at least three or four different categories of groups; we obey three or four different sets of norms and succumb to varying pressures to exhibit expected behaviour. Most of us do so unknowingly. An insight into group dynamics will, we hope, provide an insight into human behaviour—the goal of the behavioural scientist.

7.7 SUMMARY

1. A group is any number of people who interact, are psychologically aware of each other and share a group identity.

2. Individuals join groups for a variety of reasons including security, affiliation, goals, activities and attraction.

3. Groups may be categorised in a number of ways, the most important being formal, informal and reference groups.

4. Group characteristics or structure consists of cohesiveness, status, roles, norms, communication and size. It is the stable pattern of interaction between the members in relation to these characteristics that comprises group structure.

5. There are five developmental stages: forming, storming, norming, performing and adjourning.

6. Just as people have valid reasons for joining a group, they have valid reasons for wishing to remain members.

7. Groups exert tremendous pressure on their members to conform. Experiments by Asch, Milgram and Sherif highlight these pressures.

8. The Hawthorne Studies are highly influential studies of group behaviour in a work situation. Their conclusions range from establishing the Hawthorne Effect to the premise that work is a group activity.

7.8 EXAM QUESTIONS

1. With reference to a real-life social or work group discuss the elements that contribute to these people being defined as a group and not simply an aggregate of people.

2. Drawing on work by Asch, Sherif and Milgram, discuss reasons for people's apparent conformity to group pressures.

3. Discuss the part played by status in group structure.

4. Describe the five stages of group development and how knowledge of them might aid an organisational merger.

5. Describe the Hawthorne Studies and outline their implications for our understanding of groups at work.

Chapter 8

Organisations and Organisational Behaviour

Culture is a little like dropping an Alka-Seltzer into a glass—you don't see it, but somehow it does something.

Hans Magnus Enzensberger

8

Organisations and Organisational Behaviour

Learning objectives

After studying this chapter, you should be able to:

1. *Define the terms 'organisation' and 'organisational behaviour'.*

2. *Recognise three theoretical organisational perspectives.*

3. *Understand the importance of an organisational communication system and its concomitant problems.*

4. *Discuss the implications of technology within an organisation.*

5. *Evaluate the problems and solutions encountered when organisational change is introduced.*

6. *Understand two main approaches to staff recruitment, along with the concept of 'psychological contract'.*

8.1 INTRODUCTION

Up to this point we have examined the behaviour of individuals within a somewhat general environment. Now we examine the interrelationships and dynamics of humans in the business world, within corporate entities and organisations. As we shall see, organisations have their own characteristics; how these develop and interact with the workforce is the subject of much study and discussion. To understand employee behaviour we must also understand organisations, for one influences the other.

In this chapter, we examine the make-up of organisations and their ability to exist in an often-changing environment. Knowledge gained from previous chapters, in such areas as perception, learning and motivation, enhances our awareness of potential interactions between worker and organisation.

This interaction is commonly referred to as organisational behaviour. As we know, rarely, if ever, does anything occur in isolation. It is the same within organisations. We have to view them, their workforce and their environment as one. To do this we must take a Gestalt approach, that is, realise that the whole is greater than the sum of its parts.

The parts are:

(a) Human experience.

(b) Organisational experience.

(c) Interaction or interface between human and organisation.

This three-tier approach is important. We can focus on any of these parts individually, but to gain a comprehensive understanding of organisations and organisational behaviour, we must recognise that all three are interrelated.

Human experience

We understand from previous chapters how individuals, or in this case, employees:

(a) Acquire attitudes;

(b) Generate perceptions;

(c) Learn skills;

(d) Become motivated.

All of these contribute to an employee's unique perspective on her working environment and work ethos. Essentially the 'human-experience' variable refers to personal characteristics and experiences brought to the workplace by employees.

Organisational experience

This covers:

(a) Various organisational concepts.

(b) Theoretical approaches to organisations.

(c) Technology.

(d) Recruitment procedures.

These factors refer, generally, to the structure, development and operation of the company.

Interaction between human and organisation

The final tier basically refers to relationships and interactions between workers and management, including such factors as:

(a) Organisational communication.

(b) Organisational change.

(c) Psychological contract.

8.2 ORGANISATIONAL EXPERIENCE

8.2.1 What is an organisation?

An organisation is a group of people working together to attain common goals. A more complex definition offers 'a purposeful social unit of people carrying out differentiated tasks and activities which are co-ordinated by one or more managers to contribute to the organisation's goals' (Moorhead & Griffin, 1992).

A team working together to achieve a goal

Whichever definition of an organisation is used, the concept of co-ordination is implicit—to be organised is to be co-ordinated. Co-ordination is only accomplished by allowing our behaviour to be directed by others. Recognition of this fact leads individuals to voluntarily giving up some of their individual flexibility or freedom.

We can therefore say that the term 'organisation' implies a trade-off between personal independence and organisational goal achievement. How this trade-off is accomplished is the core of organisational behaviour and the focus of our chapter. We must first understand, on a broader scale, how an organisation functions.

8.2.2 Organisational concepts

An organisation is often referred to as a large group. Our knowledge of group concepts teaches us that groups have structure, development and particular characteristics. It follows therefore that organisations also possess similar attributes. Organisations are often referred to as having profiles, similar to individuals, hardworking, forward-looking, etc.

To familiarise the reader with organisational concepts, we have selected several of the most widely used, or generic, terms used in discussing organisational matters.

Organisational development: The process of planned changes and improvements through the application of behavioural-science knowledge such as learning, motivation and attitudes.

Organisational structure: The system of task reporting and authority relationships existing within an organisation, the hierarchy of authority.

Organisational culture: Core beliefs and attitudes, forming a set of values that help employees learn what is acceptable or unacceptable behaviour.

Organisational characteristics: These refer to the overall structure, culture, technology and design of the organisation.

Organisational environment: Consisting of financial resources, economic and legislative aspects outside organisational boundaries, for example 'green' legislation or EU policies.

Organisational process: This refers to processes of decision-making, creativity, communication and performance appraisal, for example delegation or shared responsibility, promotional prospects.

Organisations, regardless of size, structure or purpose, tend to share certain characteristics that facilitate smooth co-ordination and operation:

(a) Division of labour.

(b) Common goals.

(c) Hierarchy of authority.

Division of labour refers to sectionalisation or departmentalisation. Whether it is applied in the case of functional departments (such as accounting or human resources in larger companies) or to one person whose responsibility it is to buy stamps (as in a smaller company), the overall effect is similar. Workers learn expected behaviour, time is saved and expertise/knowledge is usually gained.

Common goals refers to the organisation as a whole (management and staff) possessing a shared frame of reference and a common viewpoint. The sharing of common goals provides unity of purpose, aids evaluation of functioning and promotes an individual's sense of purpose and belonging, such as achieving a new work contract over foreign competitors.

Hierarchy of authority refers to the necessity of having a recognised authority system (workers know who they have to report to) which promotes the functioning of the organisation, ensures performance and is a means of allocating status.

8.2.3 Theoretical approaches to organisations

Organisational design co-ordinates the efforts of people and departments. Designs must maximise efficiency, co-ordination and accomplishment. Three contemporary perspectives or approaches have influenced organisational design: the Classical approach, Systems approach and Human-relations approach. Each highlights a particular organisational orientation, ranging from the highly structured universal approach to the more relaxed social approach.

Classical approach

Emerging from the scientific management ethos, Classical organisation theorists, borrowing terms such as efficiency and discipline, focussed on how organisations could be structured most effectively. While scientific management centred on scientifically-controlled person-job interaction, Classical theorists centred on the concepts of logic, rationality and the efficiency of the organisation itself. They looked at how workers and management could be effectively organised into an overall structure. Key Classical theorists included Henri Fayol and Max Weber.

Weber's Bureaucracy

At the beginning of the twentieth century, German sociologist Max Weber introduced the word 'bureaucracy' into organisational language, with stability, control and predictability as the goals of any organisation. Bureaucracy offered a logical, rational and efficient *modus operandi*. Weber's view was that an administration characterised by a hierarchy of authority, rules and regulations could and would work for all organisations regardless of size. In other words, he proposed a more or less universal structure based on the assumption of efficiency.

Weber's Bureaucracy has seven basic elements devised to maximise efficiency and order among the workforce and job design. The following table describes briefly these elements:

	Elements	Comments
1.	Rules and procedures	A consistent set of rules and procedures to ensure uniform performance.
2.	Distinct division of labour	Each position to be filled by an expert.
3.	Hierarchy of authority	Clearly established chaing of command.
4.	Technical competence	Merit and competence should be based on promotion and recruitment.
5.	Segregation of ownership	Professional managers, rather than owners, should run the organisation.
6.	Rights and properties of the position	Should be associated with the organisation, not the person who holds the office.
7.	Documentation	Record of all administrative decisions, rules etc. should be kept.

Nowadays, bureaucracy tends to have negative connotations; words such as 'inflexibility' and 'red tape' are often used synonymously. Indeed, criticism of Weber's model has been widespread, including accusations of:

(a) **Rigidity,** both in structure and authority.

(b) **Impersonality,** which may lead to communication problems between employee and employer.

(c) **Ignorance of the human element:** The model does not recognise the individuality of motivation, perceptions or the principles of group behaviour.

(d) **Mechanical approach:** Workers must fit into the organisation, regardless of abilities or motivations.

Nevertheless, Classical theory remains very much the cornerstone of business organisations today. The goals of organisational order, efficiency and predictability are considered worthwhile against the backdrop of somewhat rigid authoritarian rule. Out of this approach, or perhaps because of it, a new perspective emerged, moving away from rigidity in favour of flexibility and recognising the existence of a wider organisational picture: the Systems perspective.

Systems approach

Systems theory views organisations as a set of interrelated elements functioning as a whole. It offers delegation, job enrichment and a somewhat more flexible approach to organisational design than Weber's bureaucratic structure. It is an approach conscious of the 'fit' between an organisation and its environment, looking at the Gestalt of the organisation. Implicit in this theory is the concept of open and closed organisational designs: open referring to those organisations receptive to their environment and changes in it; closed referring to those organisations tending to operate in isolation, disregarding the economic climate. This may appear contradictory in relation to the Systems theory premise; nevertheless it differs by degree rather than by design.

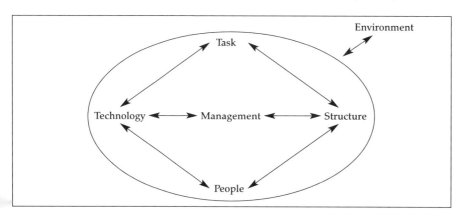

An extension of the Systems design is referred to as the Contingency approach. In many organisations, situations and outcomes are contingent upon one another. The relationship between any two variables is likely to be influenced by other existing variables. One example is how the standards of worker behaviours (outputs) is affected by the type of feedback received from society (environment) at large. If legislation forbids the pollution of air, the organisation will have to alter its inputs/transformation sections to comply. All sectors of the organisation are contingent or dependent on each other. The whole picture is a series of interacting systems.

Frequently, the Systems theory is presented as the Socio-Technical Systems theory where individual social and technical elements replace the inputs variable. Rather than putting human and material elements together, the Socio-Technical model distinguishes between them.

In effect, four systems exist:

(a) Internal social system.

(b) Internal technical system.

(c) Internal overall system with the different variables co-ordinating.

(d) The organisation as an entity co-operating with the environment, itself a system.

It is important to be aware that all four systems should be balanced; management cannot afford to sacrifice, say, the social for the technical sub-system. Researchers in the Tavistock Institute in the United Kingdom (Trist & Banforth, 1951) suggested that this had happened in the British coal mining industry, when management tried to increase productivity by reorganising work schedules and introducing new mining techniques. They failed to recognise the adverse effects this would have on the existing social system, such as breaking up long standing work groups and moving colleagues to other areas.

In an effort to overcome the problems that had arisen, the Tavistock researchers proposed the introduction of autonomous work groups.

Although co-ordinated by management, these worker groups were responsible for job assignments, training, inspection, rewards and punishment within their specific areas.

The Socio-Technical system saw management's role, not as authoritarian but as monitoring and co-ordinating both the environment and the organisation so that the two were compatible.

One of the main differences between Classical and Systems theories is that the Classical theory advocates a fairly rigid hierarchy and the other puts forward a more flexible arrangement emphasising management co-ordination.

Human-relations approach

Our third approach differs from the previous two in that it focusses exclusively on the human factor, adopting basic premises such as an individual's needs for recognition, belonging and potential for self-fulfilment. Attention shifts away from the study of human or job efficiency toward a fuller understanding of the nature of interpersonal and group relations within the organisation. Organisational orientation is characterised by a strong social emphasis.

The human relations perspective admitted to sharing the basic goal of management: to secure employee compliance with managerial authority. This is by emphasising and satisfying the needs of employees, primarily through interpersonal strategies, rather than changing the nature of the job. Perhaps the most famous study of the human relations perspective at work is the Hawthorne Studies (See in Chapter 7).

Contemporary thinking in this sphere suggests that the human relations approach is somewhat idealistic, as recognition of individual workers' needs and social wants could tie up both time and resources. For example, one individual may value having security needs met, while another may value only financial gains. This kind of difference would use valuable management time. It must be recognised that many other factors are also capable of influencing organisational behaviour, for example supervisory styles and environmental demands.

The following table summarises the three approaches from a managerial viewpoint:

Classical	Systems	Human relations
Close supervision and control.	Delegates and co-ordinates.	Makes workers feel useful and important.
Establishes work procedures and policies.	Co-ordinates social and technical systems into an integrated whole.	Allows workers to exercise self-direction and self-control.
Rigid hierarchy.	Democratic.	Attends to social factors.

Although the three perspectives differ, each possesses positive and negative points. For example, although the Classical approach is fairly rigid, the workforce has the security of knowing exactly what job they have to do and how the authority hierarchy works. The Systems approach may require complex managerial strategies to facilitate organisation-environment fit, but democratic co-ordination provides the foundation stone for the organisation. The Human Relations stance promotes interpersonal relationships and goodwill, relying on a knock-on effect to increase productivity, rather than any stringent rules or regulations.

All three perspectives share a similar aim—to enhance worker-organisation efficiency. Our next section examines a factor that compliments this efficiency, organisational technology.

8.2.4 Organisational technology

In theory, technology refers to any mechanical or intellectual process by which inputs are transformed into outputs (Moorhead and Griffin, 1992). Organisational technology refers to a successful match between an organisation's structure and its technology: in other words, its effectiveness in 'integrating technology structure, personal characteristics and social factors into a congruent goal-orientated entity' (Steers, 1993).

The introduction of new forms of technology, such as mobile phones and laptop computers, offers the possibility of new ways of working. An example of this is 'hot-desking'. Employees do not have permanent desk space and often work out of the office. When they are in the office, they move around using whatever desk space is free or which groups of people need to work together on a given day. In this way, technology offers the potential not only for new ways of thinking about office space but also for new organisational forms, as groups become more fluid and task- rather than hierarchy-based.

Technology has a profound impact on an organisation, particularly from a survival viewpoint. Developments such as the Internet also offer a challenge by changing views of market audiences and marketing strategies. Technology affects an organisation across the board, from personnel to productivity. When deciding about introducing new technology, management will often engage in the following simplified model of decision-making:

WHAT	What are the capabilities of technology?
WHY	Why would introducing technology contribute to the organisation's objectives? Will it aid management goals?
HOW	How do we successfully implement technical changes within the organisation structure?
CONSEQUENCES	Possible increase/decrease in employment. Improved skills/knowledge base. Improved quality of working life. Change in role of management. Change in levels of productivity/ profit.

Management's task is to consider the merits of new technology and how best to implement it within the overall organisational structure. From a workforce viewpoint, however, this poses a serious question: does it mean an increase in skills and knowledge or does it really mean loss of job security? Fears about job security have, in the past, proved well founded.

The introduction of new technology is fraught with problems. Will workers resent the change and refuse to co-operate? Will the technology be too costly and too advanced? Will it necessitate employing experts? In an effort to alleviate such problems, management attempts to introduce compensatory mechanisms. These processes try to overcome the negative impact of technical change. They include:

(a) Increasing employee awareness of why changes have been implemented, such as maintaining market position.

(b) Providing training courses for workers to use the new technology.

(c) Highlighting the fact that quite often the introduction of new technology enables the organisation to produce new products or services at a lower, more stable cost. This in turn increases consumer demand, resulting in increased demand for workers.

The implementation of organisational change, whether technological or structural, is potentially troublesome. See 8.3.2, where the issue has been dealt with in greater detail.

8.2.5 Organisational recruitment

Recruiting staff is now considered a highly important psychological task with far-reaching implications in areas such as finances, performance levels, staff morale and interpersonal relationships. It is important that new employees integrate well into the organisation, with co-workers, and feel in general they belong to the organisation. This matching process incorporates two common approaches to employee recruitment: Selection approach and Classification approach.

Selection approach

This is the more traditional model. The organisation attempts to match an individual with the position. The person must fit the needs of the organisation. Application forms, interviews, personality and aptitude tests are all used to find the right employee, which is time-consuming and expensive. This approach employs scientific techniques (measurement) and has two aspects:

(a) **Defining the physical, academic and psychological requirements of the job** by drawing up a job description, including the required levels of performance, psychological demands and levels of responsibility. Once important job attributes have been identified, such as initiative and flexibility, they are tested against performance criteria (how they match the doing of the job). They are then defined as the key attributes prospective candidates should possess.

(b) **Selecting individuals to match:** Companies often prefer to adopt a fairly structured interview procedure or framework involving an interview board, whose task is to assess all aspects of the interviewee. Questions asked are frequently decided beforehand with board members taking responsibility for certain areas, such as expertise, personal history. Whatever the interview structure, the interviewee will be invited to answer questions that elicit information about:

(i)   Abilities, e.g. intelligence.

(ii) Disposition, e.g. attitudes to responsibility.

(iii) Special attributes, e.g. languages, computer skills.

Although interviews are the most widely used recruitment method, their effectiveness in predicting successful job performance (known as predictive validity) varies. Loosely structured interviews, not based on a clear job and person specification, have poor predictive validity in comparison to more structured interviews.

Classification approach

This approach focusses on fitting the job to the person. The emphasis is on recruiting an individual with a proven track record. In other words, designing a job around the employee in order to make use of her best attributes. Employers concentrate on making the job attractive to the prospective employee by attending to such matters as:

(a)   Beneficial physical environment, e.g. own office, company car, pension and health contributions.

(b)   Aids to production capabilities, e.g. selection of latest technology, team back up, financial allocations—all to ease and enhance performance.

(c)   Social interaction, that the company does its best to make sure the individual is made to feel welcome and accepted.

The emphasis of this approach is on meeting the employee's expectations and demands.

Both approaches have the same goal, to ensure that the 'fit' between individual and organisation is mutually rewarding. Today, all organisations face the challenge of recruiting from and managing an increasingly diverse workforce (dual-career families, job-sharing applicants).

8.3 INTERACTION BETWEEN HUMAN AND ORGANISATIONAL BEHAVIOUR

8.3.1 Organisational communication

We all know the importance of communication. If we cannot communicate effectively, we become misunderstood, misread and eventually isolated. So what is communication? It is 'the process by which two or more parties exchange information and share meaning' (O'Reilly and Pondy, 1979). In organisational behaviour, it refers not only to the ability to communicate with supervisors and colleagues, but also the ability to recognise potential problems or barriers. The communication process in fact forms the basis of an organisation, facilitating:

(a) Interpersonal relationships.

(b) Information sharing, decision-making and feedback.

(c) Co-ordination of activities/motivation.

(d) Goal direction.

The following diagram illustrates the basic model of communication that is applicable not only to interpersonal relationships but also to organisational communication.

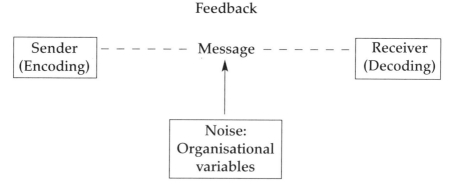

As with interpersonal relationships, an organisation faces problems if its communication system breaks down or is distorted. We summarise problems associated with each stage of our communication model.

Sender variable

(a) **Filtering/Withholding:** When sending a message, the sender may choose to filter or withhold parts. In other words, only certain sections of the message may be sent in the mistaken belief that such information is on a need-to-know basis. This course of action has two serious consequences:

(i) **Erroneous interpretation** because information scarcity may cause mistakes to be made.

(ii) **Incomplete messages** rendered meaningless to everyone except the sender.

(b) **Encoding:** The sending of messages in an understandable form. There are several points to be aware of:

(i) **Lack of common experience:** Frequently senders fail to realise that their experience is not shared by others. For example, it is no use issuing instructions on how to correct computer errors if the receiver of the message has no experience with computers.

(ii) **Semantics** are word meanings and the difference in possible interpretations of the word. For example, management may issue a work directive announcing how bad business is, employees may 'read' this as redundancies being in the pipeline.

(iii) **Jargon** is the specialised or technical language used by various professions or groups of people such as accountants or engineers. It has both positive and negative aspects from a communication point of view. Using jargon can increase efficiency and save time. If the jargon is understood by all concerned, long-winded discussions or explanations are redundant. The disadvantages or negative aspects of using jargon is that it reinforces the in-group/out-group situation. In other words, if you are not part of the in-group, jargon only serves to increase alienation.

Receiver variable

(a) **Selective attention:** Where the receiver attends to only part of the message. In other words, they select the section that they think applies to them (usually from a cue word) and consequently only attend to part of the message.

(b) **Value judgements:** When the receiver acknowledges the message to the degree to which it either reinforces or challenges their beliefs. In other words, if the message agrees with the receiver's feelings or thoughts about the topic, the value judgement will be positive. Take an annual salary review situation; if employees are informed that reviews will be low due to a downturn in production or profit levels, they proceed to make value judgements. These are made in accordance with their own perception of the situation. Depending whether perceptions agree or disagree, the statement or message will be accepted or rejected.

(c) **Credibility:** If the sender of the message is regarded in a positive light, perceived as an expert or at least to be seen to know what they are talking about. Credibility fails when workforces disregard or ridicule the sender and consequently ignore the message itself.

(d) **Overload:** Simply that too much information, either instructions or memos, is piled on the receiver, often resulting in no action.

Feedback variable

The biggest communication failure in this area is the omission of feedback to the sender. Feedback is of the utmost importance in the communication chain because it allows for clarification, verification, encouragement and motivation. It is an indication of message receipt and the degree to which it has been understood. Feedback is quite often received non-verbally, through facial expressions and body language.

Organisational variables

(a) **Noise:** Is there any disturbance within the communication network that interferes with or distorts communication, e.g. rumours, gossip, misinterpretations.

(b) **Status difference:** If the hierarchy or authority chain is rigid, communication tends to be one way, top to bottom. True communication is a two-way relationship, so organisations must be mindful that workers have the necessary feedback or a communication forum.

(c) **Time pressures/Overload:** This is similar to receiver overload. If an organisation does not allow sufficient time or space for a workforce to cope with information demands, the communication chain becomes clogged.

(d) **Communication structure:** Organisations must make sure that their communication structure is two way, so communication occurs not only top-down but also bottom-up. The workforce must perceive itself as having (and in fact does have) a forum (whether monthly meetings or more informal contact) which provides an opportunity for open communication with management.

Interestingly, according to Ralph Nicholas, as far back as 1962 (Steers, 1991) the percentage of information filtered out during downward communications amounts to approximately 80 per cent.

Percentage of information filtered in downward communications	
Top management's understanding of a message	100%
Vice president's understanding of a message	63%
General manager's understanding of a message	56%
Plant manager's understanding of a message	40%
Supervisor's understanding of a message	30%
Worker and final message	20%

When upward communication does occur, it tends to be influenced by:

(a) What the worker thinks his/her supervisor wants to know.

(b) Highlighting or exaggerating positive aspects.

(c) Omitting or downplaying negative aspects.

The basic premise of organisational communication is to provide the right information to the right person at the right time and in the right place. This sounds simple enough, but we have seen the problems that can arise. So how does an organisation avoid them? Two general routes suggest themselves:

(a) **Reduce noise:** 'Noise' blocks and distorts communication through what is generally known as the office grapevine. To overcome this, management should effectively use and monitor the grapevine to know exactly what is being said and so introduce an element of control.

(b) **Foster informal communication**: Organisations tend to have fairly structured communication patterns, but it is important to allow for flexibility. Communication must be allowed not only up down and vice versa but also horizontally. Top-down communication lends itself to issuing goals, strategies, and procedures, while upward communication lends itself to communication of problems, grievances and performance reports. Horizontal communication, on the other hand, allows for co-ordination between management and staff, as it permits intra-departmental and inter-departmental communication and problem-solving.

The communication pattern adopted by any organisation depends on many factors including:

(a) Authority structure: Autocratic or democratic.

(b) Task design: What type of business is involved.

(c) Size of organisation: Number of employees.

Four well-known communication patterns exist for organisational networks:

(a) **Wheel network**: Communication flows between the person at the end of each spoke and the person in the centre. Communication is restricted and information tends to be centralised.

(b) **Chain network**: Members communicate with those above and below but not with individuals at either end.

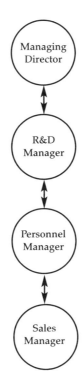

(c) **Circle network**: Each member communicates with individuals on both sides but with no one else.

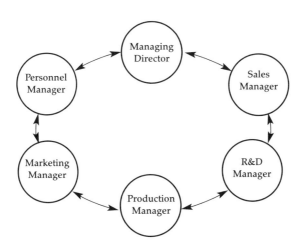

(d)   **All-channel network**: All members communicate with each other.

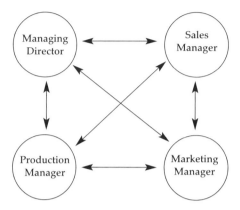

Communication is a complex and dynamic process, vital not only to effective organisational co-ordination but also to organisational achievement. It is a potentially problematic area so management must ensure that lines of communication are kept open and following.

8.3.2 Organisational change

We live in a constantly changing and dynamic environment. Not only are our thoughts, ideas and attitudes constantly being challenged but so is our working environment. Organisations also face the challenge of the environment. For example, forces of change having an effect on an organisation include:

(a)   Government/Legislation/Economy.

(b)   Financial/Human Resources.

(c)   Competitors/Markets.

Part of management's role is to recognise when some form of change is required. Triggers for organisational change tend to fall into two categories: external and internal.

External triggers

(a)   **Technological**: Artificial intelligence has meant that information is processed and disseminated more quickly. Satellite, mobile and conference phones all enhance today's communication systems; an organisation must keep abreast of improvements.

(b) **Governmental**: New consumer laws, other legislation, ecological awareness campaigns of and growing European markets drive continuous policy changes.

(c) **Economy and markets**: The sharing and opening up of European communities heightens awareness of international market trends. For example, the growing trend of large conglomerates buying out their smaller competitors emphasises the need for market vigilance.

(d) **Resource availability**: This refers to costs and availability of raw material. An unexpected price increase or unavailability of a major input (such as oil) could necessitate change.

Internal triggers

(a) **Organisational structure**: An organisation may have to be restructured, e.g. policy-making and centralisation procedures may have to be changed for the company to survive.

(b) **Organisational goals**: A change in goals may have to occur, e.g. rather than striving to be a brand leader, a company may have to diversify.

(c) **Technological**: Changes may result in replacement of part of the workforce by computers, leading to an emphasis on the recruitment of a computer-literate workforce.

Change is rarely welcomed within an organisation, yet it must occur for the company to survive. It is important that resistance, or indeed potential resistance, to change is recognised and dealt with effectively.

Schein (1985) identifies four conditions that appear to be necessary if the organisation is to be able to cope effectively with changes:

(a) **The ability to absorb and disseminate information in a reliable and valid manner:** All members of the organisation wish to receive information that is timely, accurate and trustworthy. Besides being briefed regularly by their colleagues and immediate superiors, they like to receive information from those in charge of the company on how they are coping with the latest challenges to the organisation. E-mails are often used for disseminating this level of information, as they can contain large amounts of data and not open to distortion and filtering in the way verbal messages are.

(b) **Internal flexibility and creativity to make changes that are demanded by the information obtained**: Extraordinary situations require innovative responses, and the organisation must be willing to consider alternate ways of coping with challenges it has never faced before. This may mean new work practices, or even diversifying the firm's product base.

(c) **Integration and commitment to successful attainment of the organisation's goals**: Management in organisations does not have a monopoly on the truth. It must be willing—as in the interview stage of the Hawthorne Studies in Chapter 7—to listen to all sections of the organisation when defining goals and assessing how to implement them.

(d) **An internal climate of support and freedom from threat**: Everyone in the organisation should feel that their input is not only valued, but that it will not be seen as a criticism to existing policies. Where employees feel free to make contributions, they often relate better to their colleagues, as they will be more relaxed and trusting. Many organisations foster this by encouraging their managers to have an 'open-door' policy, allowing employees to express their concerns at any time.

Change not only affects organisational structure, but also has repercussions for the workforce on a personal level. For example:

(a) **Security**: Change affects the security of employment and the day-to-day habits of the workforce, often through alteration in tasks and/or reporting relationships.

(b) **Fear of the unknown**: When change occurs people fear the worst. Questions such as, 'How will I cope?' and 'What will the new boss be like?' contribute to employee anxiety and stress and tend to result in poor performance levels.

(c) **Economic factors**: Change often has financial implications for the workforce; salaries and bonus schemes may be altered.

(d) **Social factors**: Change often breaks up the social network and group dynamics that have developed within the workforce. We are aware from our knowledge of groups (Chapter 7) how important this aspect of work is for the employee.

If change is accompanied by so much resistance, how is it possible to implement change procedures? Moorhead and Griffin (1992) suggest several strategies that management may adopt to decrease employee negativity.

(a) **Education and communication**: This centres on the open communication and supply of information and knowledge to the workforce. Once armed with knowledge, individuals automatically become less fearful and resistant. It is important that information-giving takes place before the changes occur and not afterwards.

(b) **Participation and involvement**: By involving the relevant employees in designing and planning change, resistance may be reduced. Employees may feel they have some control over the procedure.

(c) **Facilitation and support**: This refers to the emotional support and commitment given by management to employees who may experience change-related anxiety or stress in their work areas.

(d) **Negotiation and agreement**: Mutual goal-setting sessions are important in allaying fears and can only enhance change implementation.

(e) **Coercion**: Not widely recommended, as this meets resistance to change with threatened pay reductions, job losses or demotions. Such a path may be successful in the short term, but has obvious long-term negative consequences.

Change is a necessary part of life. Management must accurately assess the nature of, and the need for, change. It is also necessary for management to realise that the manner in which change is implemented is at least as important for success as the change itself.

8.3.3 Psychological contract

Traditionally, the term 'contract' in relation to employment has been thought of in legal terms. Employment contracts often explicitly outline conditions such as rates of pay, pension entitlements and number of days' holiday per year. However there are many unstated, implicit conditions that influence the employment relationship. For example, the expectation that employees will dress in a manner appropriate to the work context, that they will finish a phone call with a client rather than hang up at exactly five o'clock, or that employers will be understanding if an employee has a bereavement.

All of these kinds of expectations constitute the 'psychological contract' of employment. This is an implicit contract between employee and employer, acknowledging the employment relationship as an exchange process, involving mutual expectations and performance levels. Frequently, this type of contract is not verbalised, which may cause problems because no explicit shared frame of reference exists as to appropriate and acceptable behaviours. We refer back to 8.3.1 on the importance of open communication within organisational life.

The parties' expectations within the employment relationship may be summarised below:

Employer expectations	Employee expectations
(a) Recognition of individual rights in exchange for compliance.	(a) Rewards for outputs (salary, security).
(b) Legitimate work demands (outputs, performance).	(b) Being treated with dignity and respect.
(c) Acceptance of company objectives by employee.	(c) Acceptance of organisa-tional authority.

Organisational behaviour encompasses a broad area of study. We have addressed the fundamentals of the subject in a comprehensive manner, planning a framework from which it is possible to understand how organisations operate in today's changing and challenging environment.

8.4 SUMMARY

1. An organisation is a group of people working towards the same goals. Organisational behaviour comprises the human experience, the organisational experience and the interaction between the two.

2. Three organisational perspectives exist: Classical (rigid and somewhat authoritarian), Systems (co-ordination between social, technical and environmental aspects) and Human Relations (social dynamic) approaches.

3. Technology is vital for organisational survival. Its introduction can cause problems that must be addressed by management.

4. The Classification and Selection approaches to staff recruitment comprise respectively, job-to-human and human-to-job adjustments.

5. Communication is a vital part of organisational life. Management must be aware of potential problems and attempt solutions.

6. The concept of change can be threatening to an organisational workforce, which may offer various avenues of resistance. Management must be prepared to spend time and effort allaying fears.

7. The implicit contract between employer and employee, called the psychological contract, views employment as an exchange process.

8.5 EXAM QUESTIONS

1. Describe the features of organising.

2. Compare and contrast the management roles of each of the three organisational perspectives.

3. Discuss internal and external triggers of change for an organisation.

4. Describe potential remedies for breakdowns/barriers in the communication process.

5. What is the 'psychological contract'?

Chapter 9

Culture and Society

The human being is immersed right from birth
in a social environment which affects him just as much
as his physical environment. Society, even more,
in a sense, than the physical environment, changes
the very structure of the individual, because it not only
compels him to recognise facts, but also provides him
with a ready made system of signs, which modify his thought.

Jean Piaget (1966)

9

Culture and Society

Learning objectives

After studying this chapter, you should be able to:

1. *Understand the importance of culture and society in relation to individual behaviour.*

2. *Define and describe the characteristics and components of culture.*

3. *Describe and evaluate the socialisation process.*

4. *Evaluate the mechanisms of society in shaping human behaviour.*

5. *Discuss the concept of social class and its place within society.*

9.1 INTRODUCTION

In the preceding chapters we have studied human behaviour on an individual level (attitudes, motivation and perception) and at group level (groups and organisations). To understand human behaviour more fully, we must place our observations in a wider context and examine the influence on behaviour of cultural and societal rules. This chapter presents an overview or 'Gestalt' of the human condition, adding to the picture of factors influencing human behaviour.

Nineteenth-century psychologist William James suggested that the world into which the newborn infant comes could be likened to a 'booming, buzzing confusion', as all sights and sounds are completely new. In growing up, infants must learn to translate this 'confusion' into a lifestyle within their own culture. The diagram on the next page represents the interaction of variables that play a part in this learning process.

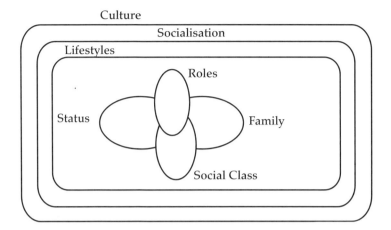

For simplicity, this chapter is divided into two parts. The first examines culture: how it is absorbed, passed down from generation to generation and influences our collective behaviours. The second part identifies society and its powerful influences through mechanisms such as norms, roles and lifestyles. Together, culture and society play an important role in shaping our behaviours.

9.2 CULTURE

Culture is difficult to define. One definition offered by Kluckholm (1951) notes that culture is 'the distinctive way of life of a group of people, their complete design for living'. In other words, culture is shared by a group of people, is learned, distinctive and involves a lifestyle. Sociologists often refer to culture as the totality of those human attitudes, values, beliefs and mechanisms (mental and physical) that represent a life pattern of a particular group or society.

9.2.1 Expressions of culture

Cultures are often differentiated by means of national boundaries. In today's ever-changing world, national boundaries are fast disappearing, and rather than allow cultures or lifestyles to disappear, people are clinging more strongly to the roots of their cultural identity. It has become common practice for emigrants to bring particular aspects of their culture to their adopted homelands. We see this happening, for example, within Asian communities in Britain where arranged marriages are still very much in evidence. In recent years, this is evident in Ireland also, as small ethnic groups attempt to establish some sense of identity in this country. Transporting culture provides the new immigrants with a sense of continuity and security in what is often a vastly different and hostile land.

9.2.2 Subcultures

Subcultures are evident worldwide. Once subsumed within the prevalent culture, they are now becoming increasingly noticeable as people retain much of their original lifestyles and customs. We have deliberately highlighted the nationalistic element of subcultures, as it tends to be the most easily recognised. It is important to realise that subcultures also exist in:

(a)   Religion (Hindus, Muslims).

(b)   Age (youth, elderly).

(c)   Sexual orientation (heterosexual, homosexual).

People, belonging to a subculture, whatever its make-up, feel a sense of identity and belonging.

When different subcultures cohabit or live together, this is seldom achieved without problems, as when racism occurs. We see evidence of this in Germany, for example, where Turkish immigrants are continuously harrassed by ultra right-wing nationalistic forces. In Britain, Asians are targetted by extremists from the National Front. On our own island, racism occurs in nationalist and loyalist murders and as attacks on minority immigrant groups.

9.2.3 Characteristics of culture

All cultures possess characteristics or distinctive features:

(a)   **Culture is learned:** We absorb aspects of culture. For example, the effect of Catholicism is deeply rooted within the Irish psyche, as are the notions of superstition and fatalism. In a desire to be at one with their adoptive homelands, emigrants often willingly take on and learn indigenous ideologies and values. This was certainly the case at the beginning of the century when thousands flocked to New York with the sole aim of becoming an 'American'.

(b)   **Culture serves the needs of society:** Culture provides a sense of continuity and structure for societies. For much the same reasons as people join groups, culture fulfils the needs of identity, security and affiliation. We can see many Irish people using the Irish spelling of their names, speak the Irish language at home, and placing their children in Irish-speaking schools.

(c) **Culture is cumulative and adaptive:** Culture is an accumulation of customs, rituals, beliefs and values, with each new era adding to this cultural storehouse. It is also adaptive, responding albeit slowly to shifts of belief and opinion within society. We can see the difference between today's Ireland and Éamon De Valera's ideal Ireland of the 1930s.

9.2.4 Components of culture

The components of culture provide mechanisms through which society's well-being and continuance are ensured. The expression of these components reflects the state of society. For example:

Institutions

Institutions provide an organised system of behavioural rules or norms for a society, such as:

(a) **Conventions:** These are appropriate patterns of behaviour in any given situation. They are society's unwritten rules for acceptance and appropriate behaviour: for example, all forms of social etiquette. The penalties for transgression of conventions are slight and often waived.

(b) **Mores:** These are strong moral sanctions. They are the most important social norms of behaviour covering areas such as fidelity in marriage, the forbidding of incest and murder, and the recognition of immoral acts. Mores tend to be codified in law (as with forbidding murder and incest).

(c) **Laws:** These formal recognitions of appropriate and inappropriate behaviours reflect society's views at any particular time and exist to ensure the continuance and well-being of society. It is important to realise that laws do change, usually reflecting a change in cultural ideas and mores. For example, it is no longer unlawful for a man to marry his dead wife's sister.

Ideas

Culture, because it is adaptive, recognises the necessity of adopting an era's values, beliefs and attitudes. Values within in a society provide standards of comparison for its people. For example, Irish culture stresses the value of family life. Beliefs refer to states of knowledge. The beliefs of the Irish nation used to be very much intertwined with Catholicism and nationalism, but over the past twenty years there have been many changes in our cultural beliefs and values.

Youth culture is constantly changing.

Materials

Materials may be described as the physical expressions of the human state. They form the link between a culture's knowledge base and its artefacts or tools, such as arts, literature and technology. Culture is frequently expressed through the arts.

Every culture has its own songs and poetry providing its people with a sense of the past. Ireland has its traditional music and England its folk songs. We can also see shifts in culture, through the introduction and use of new material artefacts, such as the growing availability of the Internet in Irish homes.

Culture reflects, at any given time, the state of society.

9.3 SOCIETY

To survive, individuals must learn to live in harmony; to do this, they must recognise, understand and adopt acceptable behavioural patterns. This process is known as socialisation.

9.3.1 Socialisation

Socialisation may be defined as the process of learning to live in a society by adopting socially acceptable behaviour. It is the means by which society prepares individuals for the role/s they are expected to play, whether personal, work or social. The culture in which an individual lives determines how this socialisation process develops.

Basically socialisation has two main functions:

(a) It prepares people for their place in society, from teaching a child necessary life skills to learning what is acceptable and appropriate behaviour.

(b) It ensures the continuity of society: individuals must perpetuate conventions, mores and beliefs in an effort to pass behaviour patterns from generation to generation.

9.3.2 Agencies of socialisation

It is hard to think of an area of our lives untouched by the process of socialisation. Even if we choose not to interact with other people we are in fact still choosing a form of socialisation—that of avoidance. The principal agencies from which we learn socialisation skills are:

(a) **Family:** The family is the strongest socialisation agency. We learn how to cope, share and adjust to life. The familial influence can exert itself into adulthood, affecting life decisions such as choice of career, marriage partners, etc. The family is our first introduction into society (the society of our siblings and extended family) and subconsciously we adopt its value system. It serves as a base for later independent functioning and as a touchstone for influencing the development of new relationships.

(b) **School:** After the family, we spend most of our formative years in primary and secondary education. Here we get the opportunity to mix with other people, affording us a different perspective on the behaviours and beliefs experienced to date. School is also the setting in which the State first has a chance to influence individuals through its interpretation of the curriculum subjects. It is a potent force in the socialisation of children, inculcating them with societal attitudes.

(c) **Peer groups:** These are groups of people with whom we identify. They could be friends, work colleagues or associates possessing similar interests, for example sports clubs, charities or political groupings. Though the amount of time spent with peer groups is less than with family and school, peer groups still have influence on us; note teenagers' strict adherence to dress codes (e.g. combats) and certain types of music (e.g. garage).

(d) **Mass media:** In this context mass media refers to the organised means of information transmission through a medium such as newspapers, magazines, television, radio or cinema. It is an extremely powerful agency, presenting people with an abundance of varied lifestyles, beliefs and values. Regardless of age, mass media continues to exert a strong influence on the way we perceive our role within society.

9.3.3 Mechanisms of socialisation

How do we learn socially acceptable behaviours? As we develop through childhood, we learn and absorb the rules of appropriate or inappropriate actions. Our behaviour, frequently monitored by family and school, is shaped into a pattern that conforms to society's rules. This process does not stop; throughout our lives we are constantly adapting our behaviours to 'fit in' with the social situation we find ourselves in. Society's main mechanisms for shaping behaviour are:

(a) **Imitation:** A young child learns to cope with her environment by imitating her parents. We learn how to act in social settings by imitating the behaviour of those around us, for example learning table manners, showing respect to others.

(b) **Conditioning:** This term was referred to in the context of Behaviourist learning theory (see section 3.2), in which appropriate behaviour was rewarded and inappropriate behaviour punished. In the same way, our behaviour is conditioned by society's reaction. Approval may be in the form of encouragement, attention and praise, while disapproval may be ostracism, verbal criticism or silence. Similar behavioural treatments from our family or peer groups can also condition our behaviour until we learn to display appropriate and acceptable behaviour.

(c) **Identification**: Just as we join certain groups reflecting our views, we also identify with people we feel are similar to ourselves. The most obvious people we identify with are our parents. As we grow older, we adopt perceived correct behaviours according to how we identify with people such as peers, work colleagues and friends.

9.3.4 Norms

To survive and set standards of behaviour, society has evolved its own mechanism for survival, called norms. These important rules of behaviour fulfil two basic functions, they:

(a) **Set the standard of behaviour**, dictating what behaviour is acceptable and expected, for example when meeting a new acquaintance the norm is to shake hands.

(b) **Ensure continuity**, so that certain rules of behaviours are repeated by individuals in the same kind of situations.

Norms guide an individual to fit into society and are central to another important aspect of socialisation process, roles.

9.3.5 Roles

A role may be defined as a pattern of behaviour expected in a specific position, such as teacher, mother, son. We enact several different roles in everyday life, each being relevant to a specific social situation. For example, at the moment you are probably in the role of student, during coffe break you are a friend, and at home you may be wife, husband, sister, daughter or son. We adopt what we perceive are the behavioural expectations of the role we are playing. For example, our behaviour in the role of friend is often different from our behaviour in the role of daughter or son.

Not only do we adopt and enact role expectations, but so do others; that is to say, others perceiving our behaviour in a specific role often psychologically assess what they would do in similar circumstances. If role perceptions are similar there are no problems, but if perceptions differ, conflict is inevitable. At work, for example, an employee who adopts what she considers appropriate behaviour for an assistant may be at odds with her employer, for the sole reason that the employer has different expectations and perceptions of the same role.

Conflicts within role behaviour take two patterns:

(a) **Inter-role conflict**: Where performance in one role interferes with performance in another, for example a Garda may find that his behaviour at work runs over into his family life and he becomes very autocratic.

(b) **Intra-role conflict**: Where conflicting demands of different requirements of the role lead to role ambiguity (confusion) and/or role incompatibility. An example of this could be where an employee is called on to use her initiative, yet is taken to task for not asking permission.

Whatever role we adopt at any given time is, or has been, shaped by societal approval. The diagram below displays a simple model of role adoption.

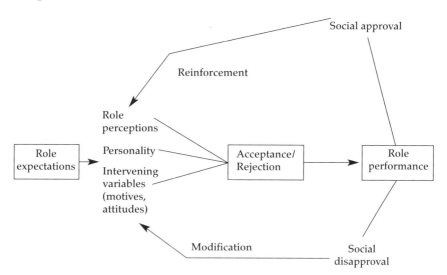

9.3.6 Social class

Social class is difficult to define. Forms of social stratification exist in all societies. One form is social class, other forms include caste, tribe etc. One definition offered by Schiffman and Kanuk (1997) proposes social class as 'a division of members of a society into a hierarchy of distinct status classes, so that members of each class have relatively the same status and members of all other classes have either more or less status'. In other words, social class is a collection of individuals sharing similar lifestyles and recognising a differentiation between their group and others. This differentiation is regarded as hierarchical, spanning from low to high.

Social class serves as a frame of reference for members and non-members alike, and is perpetuated by the following means:

(a) **Class consciousness**: Members of a class are conscious of the existence of shared values, attitudes and beliefs within each class and between social classes.

(b) **Uniformity of lifestyle**: Members within a social class share similar lifestyles, adhering to social expectations, such as occupation, education, income levels.

(c) **Patterns of social interaction**: Members share similar behaviour patterns, such as areas of social intercourse, leisure interests, holidays and residential geography.

9.3.7 Status

Intertwined within the notion of class differentiation is the concept of status. The amount of status possessed by a class often defines that the place of that class in the social hierarchy. Status may be ascribed (given) or achieved (sought) and is often defined in terms of:

(a) Wealth/income.

(b) Power.

(c) Education.

(d) Occupation.

These socio-economic variables are recognised and accepted within the class hierarchy as indicators of class positioning. Simply, status is a social-identity marker placing people in relation to others.

As we have learned, culture and society shapes behaviour, beliefs and values. All cultures possess similar characteristics and components, but each is unique in its expression. Our final chapter gives the reader an opportunity to decide and assess the influence of the unique forces contributing towards an 'Irish culture'.

9.4 SUMMARY

1. Culture is the distinctive way of life of a group of people, is learned, serves the needs of society and is cumulative and adaptive.

2. Components of culture comprise institutions (convention, mores and laws), ideas (beliefs, attitudes and values) and materials (technology, arts and literature).

3. The socialisation process prepares an individual for society through the agencies of family, school, peers and the media.

4. Mechanisms of society provide a learning framework for appropriate behavioural expressions.

5. Society's norms, roles and social-class structures enhance an individual's sense of belonging and identity.

9.5 EXAM QUESTIONS

1. Define 'culture' and describe its characteristic features.

2. With reference to components of culture such as conventions, ideas and materials, describe how you think Irish culture has changed in the past twenty years.

3. 'Culture is an organising and stabilising influence. It not only encourages and discourages particular behaviour ... but also allows people to understand and anticipate the behaviour of others in that culture.' Bernstein et al., 1994. (MII, 1998).

4. Describe what is meant by the term 'role'. What potential disadvantages are there in adopting a particular role?

5. Social class has been described as a 'social identity matter'. Would you agree?

Chapter 10

Trends in Irish Social Change

All changed, changed utterly:
A terrible beauty is born.

W. B. Yeats (1865-1939)

10

Trends in Irish Social Change

Learning objectives

After studying this chapter, you should be able to:

1. *Present the main demographic changes in Ireland over the last fifty years, especially the effect of industrialisation on social class, the family and the distribution of population within the State.*

2. *Explain the way in which Irish marriage and fertility rates have changed over the last fifty years, and how they compare to the EU average.*

3. *Describe briefly what is meant by social class in the Irish context, how it has been affected by industrialisation and how mobile groups are within it.*

4. *Explain what is meant by the dependency ratio, what effect it has on the Irish economy and how it is affected by the present age profile in Ireland.*

5. *Outline and describe the main trends in Irish development over the last fifty years which have shaped today's Irish society.*

10.1 INTRODUCTION

In many European countries the past exerts a strong 'pull' on its inhabitants, with events of many years ago still influencing how they act. This is no less true of Ireland. Our past still holds sway over our consciousness and institutions. The reasons for this are many, and are the stuff of both cliché and historical fact.

Recently, there have been profound changes in the economic and social make-up of Irish society. The foundation for these changes is the social, economic and political events and decisions of the mid- to late twentieth century. Rather than being now irrelevant to our analysis, they are important as a starting point for what has happened in the late 1990s and early 2000s.

Few people anticipated Ireland developing from an economically weak nation to a country able to boast one of the highest rates of growth in the EU. This economic boom—known as 'the Celtic tiger economy'—has not been without its downside. The Yeats' phrase 'terrible beauty' quoted at the beginning of the chapter was about the cataclysmic changes for Irish society brought about by the 1916 Rising; with the profound social and economic changes of the late twentieth and early twenty-first century, a new type of terrible beauty has been born. The challenges that remain for Irish society, especially greater inclusiveness for economically deprived elements, are dealt with in later sections.

As well as fiscal achievement, Ireland has finally achieved some form of stability in Northern Ireland with the Good Friday agreement, and the economic and political outlook has never looked as positive.

In this chapter we present a very brief overview of Irish society during the last fifty years or so. We stress that it is an overview; because of this we have simplified and in some cases omitted sociological conceptual models. We supply references at the end of the book that may provide you with some sources for further examination of this topic. Causes for change in Irish society range from our admission into the (then) EEC, through our increasing industrialisation to the lessening of the influence of the Catholic Church. It is important to note that the sociological changes in Irish society are seldom simple and are often the result of complex, long-standing and interactive social forces, such as demography, fertility and nuptiality (marriage). We will conclude with some suggestions as to how we believe the country will develop in the twenty-first century.

It should be kept in mind that in this chapter 'Ireland' and 'Irish society' refers only to the Republic of Ireland. This is for practical reasons as the two Irish entities (north and south) have developed separately and differently over much of the twentieth century. The first section will examine the background to change within Irish society.

10.1.1 Background to change in Irish society

As Rottman and O'Connell (1982) state, in their article on the changing Irish social structure, Irish society was predominately rurally based for the main part of the twentieth century. This meant that large numbers of Irish workers were employed on the land, whether on their own farms, as workers on other people's farms, or as agricultural suppliers of some sort. With the advent of industrialisation this changed, as we will see later in the chapter.

Another fundamental change has been in the position of the Catholic Church in Irish society, as described in a Breen *et al.* (1990) article on religion and the State. A papal nuncio once described Ireland as the most Catholic country in the world, and this was reflected in the fact that Irish social legislation mirrored the Church's position on most social issues. This has altered in the last thirty-five years or so, with particularly significant changes, and attempted changes, from the late 1980s to the present day. Such changes have had a knock-on effect on the structure of the Irish family as noted by Kennedy (1986 and 2001). These changes—particularly the passing of a divorce referendum in 1995—displayed the diminishing power of the Catholic Church over Irish citizens and legislators.

Lastly, as a background to Irish society, the eventual admission of Ireland to the EEC (now the European Union and formerly also the EC) has led to the implementation of economic and social directives, which have forced changes in every section of Irish society. We will briefly examine these below in evaluating how they have affected the course of Irish society since our accession to membership in 1973.

10.2 THE DEMOGRAPHY OF IRISH SOCIETY

Demographics is the study of population, including the age, sex and distribution of the people in a country. One important aspect of this is movement, usually within the confines of a particular state. It includes such things as migration (movement within a state), emigration (movement out of a state) and immigration (movement into a state). This section will discuss the demography of the Irish state during the last fifty years or so.

Main population centres in Ireland.

From the early nineteenth century until the early 1990s, Ireland has had a reputation for large-scale emigration of its population to countries with a greater supply of employment. This has been the most characteristic and best-known demographic factor in Irish society. However, it obscures the very important and often contributory factor of migration. In looking at the period in question, we first examine the reasons for, and effect of, migration on Irish society.

Up to and including the 1950s, the Irish economy was highly dependent on trade with Britain, and Ireland's fortunes often mirrored those of Britain. Ireland was a hostage to the state of the British economy. The 1950s were a particularly bad time for the Republic, with a severely depressed Irish economy and very large emigration to Britain and elsewhere. In 1958, through the First Programme for Economic Expansion, the Irish government tried to lessen its reliance on Britain by attracting investment from foreign multinationals and embracing the increasing industrialisation spreading throughout the Western world.

The result of the First and Second Programmes for Economic Expansion (the latter in 1964) was the setting up of bodies such as the Industrial Development Authority, the National Economic and Social Council, and the Economic and Social Research Institute in the late 1950s and early 1960s. The two National Expansion programmes tried to combat the large-scale emigration and unemployment. These efforts were to have a major effect on migration patterns within the Republic, particularly the concentration of population on the eastern seaboard. Industrial development in the eastern region of Ireland (Meath, Kildare, Wicklow, and Dublin) led to a large population movement to that area to fill the jobs being created. By the 1980s, 30 per cent of the nation's population would live in this area surrounding the capital.

Since this time, even with concerted governmental policies to decentralise state offices and departments, the concentration of population around the Dublin region has not been reduced. In fact, Central Statistics Office figures released in 2001 suggested that the upward trend in Dublin's population will continue, while population in the Midlands continues to decrease.

The population explosion in the Greater Dublin area and its surrounding counties led to burgeoning satellite towns (for example

Tallaght, Finglas) and to the decline of the inner-city areas of Dublin and other cities. The net effect was that groups such as teenagers, single people and the economically deprived were more likely to migrate. This movement led to a reduction in the numbers working in agriculture (see the table below, cited in Kennedy (2001). As a consequence, the importance of this sector for Irish culture and the economy has decreased. This migration pattern is in line with other European countries, but as Courtney (1982) noted, was low by international standards.

Numbers working in agriculture, industry and services, 1926-2000					
Year	Agriculture (000s)	Industry (000s)	Services (000s)	Total (000s)	Unemployed (000s)	Labour force (000s)
1926	653	162	406	1,220	79	1,300
1946	568	225	432	1,225	64	1,289
1971	272	320	457	1,049	61	1,110
1981	196	363	587	1,146	126	1,272
1986	168	301	606	1,075	227	1,302
1996	136	351	798	1,285	190	1,475
2000 (Nov)	123	499	1,088	1,710	68	1,778

Source: Kennedy, Giblin and McHugh, 1988, Labour force Survey, 1996 and Central Statistics Office (C.S.O.), 2000.

Though the actual numbers in farming are decreasing annually, the economic, political and emotional power of the farming community has not diminished. If we consider the way that large numbers of the urban, as well as rural, Irish population voluntarily gave up work and recreational activities in 2001 during the outbreak of foot and mouth disease, we can see a society which still places importance on the farming community.

10.2.1 Emigration

For many people, the spectacle of emigration is more emotive and often of greater concern than the less-mentioned migration. At the beginning of the period we are examining—the 1950s—there was a great deal of emigration from Ireland to Britain and other countries. The problem of emigration was examined by the Commission on Emigration in 1955, and attempts were made to alleviate it by the First and Second Commissions for Economic Expansion (1958 and 1964).

The nature of Irish emigration since the economically depressed 1950s has been quite cyclical. Certain periods of net emigration (more people emigrating than immigrating) tend to be followed by periods of net immigration (more people immigrating than emigrating). The determining factor in net immigration or emigration has been the economic health of Ireland and its business partners. Irish accession to the (then) EEC brought subsidies and grants to sustain and improve farming and infrastructure, and led to a lessening of our dependence on the British economy.

The 'story' of Irish emigration states that there was net emigration in the 1950s and 1960s; a positive economic climate (perhaps due to accession to the EEC) led to net immigration in the 1970s; the 1980s was, in the main, high net emigration, while in the late 1990s there has been a large increase in both the population and the net immigration figures.

Tansey (1998) succinctly sums up the Irish experience with emigration since the 1950s:

> The relationship between employment performance and population change is striking. The sharp fall in total employment during the 'hungry '50s' caused a steep rise in net emigration, culminating in the population falling to its lowest ever level in 1961. In contrast, employment expansion during the 1970s caused net immigration into the country, inducing significant population gains between 1971 and 1979.
>
> More recently, the jobs boom of the 1990s has reversed the heavy net emigration that characterised the middle and late 1980s. Instead of net emigration, there has been substantial net immigration into Ireland. Between 1992 and 1997, immigrants exceeded emigrants by over 23,000. In the year to April 1997, net immigration amounted to 15,000 people, underpinning the largest annual increase in Ireland's population since 1982.

Irish economic indicators point to a continuation of this trend as emigrants return home from abroad and foreign and non-EU nationals take up the jobs and careers which have developed due to the expansion in employment opportunities in foreign, multinational high-technology companies, among others, setting up in Ireland. The CSO figures for April 2000 give the net immigration figure as approximately 20,000 people per year, with a population of 3.79 million.

The population figure is the highest since the population census of 1881 and the highest in the history of the state. Though it is discussed widely in the media, non-EU nationals only accounted for 18 per cent (or 8,000 people) of the immigration figure. This is not to underplay the importance of the debate on the treatment of asylum seekers and economic migrants.

A reflection of the strength of the Irish economy can be seen from the fact that the level of unemployment in Ireland in 2001 stood at 3.7 per cent, and many economists referred to this as 'full employment'. It remains to be seen if Ireland has indeed become a new economy, as some commentators suggest, or whether the cyclical levels of net emigration will return when the economy is faced with weaker world economic conditions. With record levels of government revenue funding long overdue infrastructure development and with levels of current debt effectively removed, it would seem that Ireland has left behind the economic 'bad old days' of the 1980s.

A great deal of Ireland's economic expansion is attributable to the success of the IDA (Irish Development Agency) and other agencies in attracting inward technology investors such as Dell, IBM and Intel. Continued stability in employment depends on the success of these employers (some of the largest in the private sector) as well as the ability of the Irish government to attract more investment.

In its favour, Ireland has a well-educated workforce and a tax-friendly environment—the reason why the technology companies invested here in the first place. Since 1987, this has been underpinned by a series of three-yearly national partnership agreements. At first, these aimed (in the form of the Programme for National Recovery) to regulate pay increases; now it involves the Government and the social partners (the unions, the business organisations and the farming community, to name a few) agreeing on broad fiscal issues.

In spite of the success of these partnership agreements, the Government has to cope with persistent levels of long-term unemployment, which tend to be localised in areas of high poverty and deprivation. These people in turn tend to suffer from high levels of migration and emigration, especially when economic conditions are unfavourable.

The type of people who are likely to suffer long-term unemployment and have to emigrate has changed from what Breen and Whelan (1996) call the 'traditional stereotype' of male, largely unskilled emigrants possessing poor manual skills to:

> The mid-1980s [when] the migratory flow appeared to be broadly representative of the structure of Irish society with less indication than in earlier periods of any marked predominance by any one particular social group. ... Any slight imbalance which now exists appears to involve above average flows by those from higher social groups with the outflow rate among those with third-level qualifications being significantly greater than the national average.

Breen and Whelan go on to point out that those from educationally disadvantaged lower socio-economic groups are more likely to migrate due to 'push' factors, whereas those from the better educated middle classes will often migrate due to 'pull' factors.

Having examined Ireland's demographic aspects of migration, we will next look at some of the reasons contributing to Ireland's traditionally idiosyncratic population structure in terms of fertility and nuptiality (marriage).

10.3 FERTILITY AND NUPTIALITY

Due to the importance of land in Irish society and the succession rights controlling it, Ireland has had a traditionally late marriage age and a high level of celibacy. The daughters in a family were often married off with a dowry, and those sons who would not inherit the family land often emigrated. Even those who did inherit land often waited until both parents had died to marry. As it was often common that the mother was some years younger than the father, the sons were into middle age before they married. The cycle of late marriage became a self-perpetuating phenomenon.

Other traditional factors were high levels of marital fertility (meaning the number of children born to each marriage). As only the eldest son inherited, the others had to seek a living either in the locality (of which there was little chance), in the industrialised eastern part of the country, or by emigrating.

The changes that have occurred in the last five decades have been gradual and complex they could hardly have been foreseen. They have radically altered the fertility and nuptiality patterns within Irish society.

Between the years 1961 and 1981 there was a drop in marital fertility in Ireland. Courtney (1982) suggests that the reason for this lies in the fact that:

(a) During this period there were **substantial occupational changes** from agriculture into production and service industries, coupled with increasing regional development and urbanisation. This had the effect of more people moving from the land, and from the implicit acceptance they would adopt traditional roles within marriage.

(b) There was an **increase in the number of married women within the workforce.** Up until 1973, there was what was known as the 'Civil Service ban' on married women in the workforce. When women who worked in certain occupations married, they had to resign their job and stay in the home. This situation first showed signs of changing in the late Sixties (1967) when banks removed the ban on married women working. The real catalyst, however, was Ireland's accession to the EEC in 1973 and its equality directives that were subsequently adopted. These changed society's perceptions of women—and women's rights—in the workplace.

(c) The **changes in the law on contraception** came at a time when there had been a recent re-stating of the Catholic Church's views on contraception in the encyclical *Humanae Vitae* (1967). This combined with the increasingly vocal views of feminists, exemplified by Germaine Greer (1967), who contended that women could only have control over their lives when they had control over their fertility.

It was in this atmosphere of change and the questioning of moral values that a concerted campaign began to force a change in the

Republic's anti-contraception laws. Campaigners had long been making frequent and well publicised trips to buy contraceptives in Northern Ireland, which had more liberal contraception laws. By openly showing contempt for the law banning the import of contraceptives, they aimed to goad the Republic's authorities into changing legislation on contraception.

The McGee case (1973) came to the Supreme Court where Mrs McGee argued through her lawyers that the law should be interpreted to allow contraceptives to be imported. Mrs McGee won her case and the Government was forced to bring a bill before the Oireachtas providing for the import of contraceptives. This bill (1973) and the subsequent 1979 Act restricted the availability of contraceptives to married couples, when prescribed by a medical practitioner. It was only in 1986 that chemists were authorised to supply contraceptives. The subsequent 1992 and 1993 Acts led to the provision of vending machines for condoms and a lowering of the age at which people could be prescribed or sold contraceptives. All of this has contributed to a drop in the birth rate.

As Kennedy (1986) points out in her article on the family, **the increasing influence of television** on our lives and the greater receptivity of ideas due to membership of the EEC meant that people in Ireland began to live differently. Further, they began to embrace different moral values from those advocated by the Catholic Church. This has led, among other things, to a increase in the number of children born outside marriage and to an increase in the number of couples prepared to live together without being married. Some estimates put the number of children born outside marriage at approximately thirty percent of all children born in the state. This percentage has increased slowly over the ten years to 2001 and was still in single-digit percentage figures as late as the early 1980s.

Even though our pattern of fertility and nuptiality is now more typical of the European norm, Courtney (1982) was still able to state that the Irish pattern was 'still quite distinctive' in that the average age on marriage and average family size was still higher than our European neighbours. Kennedy (2001) puts this in the following terms:

> For much of the twentieth century family patterns in Ireland differed from those in other European countries. Analysis based on marriage, birth and fertility rates, at intervals across the century,

could lead to the conclusion that the Irish experience was unique.

And qualifies this by saying that:

> ...while, in many respects, family change in Ireland constitutes a special case, it has followed a path similar to other European countries.

The period since 1980 has seen more and more Irish women in the workforce. Allied to increasing availability and use of contraception, this has led to a lowering of the fertility of Irish women. The latest CSO report, in 1998, showed the Irish fertility rate at 1.91 children per woman (see table below). This was still higher than the European average of 1.44 (with the UK at 1.70 and Germany at 1.30), though fertility levels were significantly lower than before and would seem to be moving away from traditionally high patterns. The highest fertility rate in Europe is now Iceland at 2.09.

Foley (1998) presents figures to suggest that in the last two years births have once again begun to increase—to above the 50,000 mark—but she remarks that the rate is still below that needed to keep the population at its present level. This would require a fertility rate of 2.1 children per woman.

Total fertility rate for 1960 to 1998	
Year	Total Fertility Rate (TFR)
1960	3.76
1970	3.87
1980	3.23
1990	2.12
1998	1.93
Source: CSO	

The reasons for this change in fertility are given above: essentially, these are women's greater participation in the workforce and wider access to and use of contraception. Add to this analysis the fact that unmarried women account for approximately thirty per cent of children born in the State and you have what Whelan (1994) refers to as 'the paradoxical nature' of Irish values. That is it say, an apparently Catholic nation which narrowly passes a divorce referendum (in 1995), yet still has high mass attendance rates (even if these are falling) and strongly conservative input into many of its social debates 'on questions of abortion or sexual freedom' (Whelan, 1994). Dillon (1998) suggests that the change in the status of divorce 'seems to be indicative of people's ability to tolerate pluralism'.

Regarding previous differences between Ireland and its European partners, Whelan (1994) comments:

> In relation to married women's participation in the labour market and certain forms of unmarried parenthood, Irish views are quite typical of liberal European patterns.

The statistic concerning children born outside of marriage points to the fact that marriage as an institution for the raising of a family may not be as important as before. The lower number of children born to each woman in the State also suggests—in the words of Whelan (1994) that:

> ... Irish patterns of family values represent a 'pick-and-mix' approach, which blends a variety of traditional and modern value positions together to form a distinctive alternative.

Patterns of fertility and nuptiality have changed quite an amount since the early 1980s, though there are still some conservative views and practices in this regard. The change in attitudes towards the family can be evidenced in the fact that the marriage rate (of 4.5 per thousand) has fallen to below that of the EU average of 5.1 per thousand (Foley, 1998). This should be considered alongside the fact that more couples now live together in Ireland without getting married.

Fertility and nuptiality changes in Irish society have exerted strong pressures on the Irish family. As well as changes in contraception, changes in the Civil Service ban on working wives and EC equality directives, there is now a recognition on the part of the State of the role of women in society. This has helped to allow women the choice of working inside or outside the home and, as Kennedy (1986) remarks, has substantially changed the nature of the family in Ireland.

The Irish family has not been immune to the pan-European sociological change from extended to nuclear family, but it has received little or no state support in line with the State's constitutional prerogative to do so (Kennedy, 1986). This, in addition to the industrialisation of the last fifty years, means that the Irish family is not the primary unit of socialisation it used to be.

In section 10.6 we will examine how decreased fertility and economic affluence have affected what is of great concern to many governments around Europe: the dependency ratio.

10.4 SOCIAL CLASS

This section will examine the effect social class has had on Irish society in the last fifty years and the way in which social-class structure has been affected by the changes discussed above; for example, has industrialisation transformed the class structure? More importantly, we examine how much social mobility the class system allows its members, whether they move upwards or downwards.

Social class is a term used to describe an individual according to his/her income level or interests. Nevertheless, it is an emotive term because the suggestion that someone is from a particular social class often has negative resonances and implications. In the popular consciousness, the term 'social class' is often associated with landed aristocratic privilege and its opposite, the urban unemployed. Social class is a more pervasive, subtle and persistent concept than this. It is a term which can be used to describe groupings for people's attitudes, interests and lifestyles as well as for people's economic 'life chances'.

Breen *et al.* (1990) put it as follows:

> The social-class structure represents the way in which the distribution of resources for economic participation is organised in a society. A social class thus consists of families that possess similar packages of resources that can be used to generate income. Understanding a social-class structure presents two problems:
>
> (i) Identifying the set of positions that are available for economic participation—the 'empty places' which individuals can fill—and,

(ii) Specifying the mechanisms by which individuals are recruited or allocated to places within that set of positions.

It is these economic life chances, or 'packages of resources' which are of concern here. In particular, have they changed with economic affluence? A further part of the question is related to the concept of social mobility, which refers to the ability to move between social classes. Some societies have high social mobility and it is relatively easy for individuals within them to move between classes. Social mobility and social class are strongly related, as low social mobility will mean a more rigid class system, and vice versa.

10.4.1 Social class: preserving the status quo?

In his article on social class Whelan (1985) seeks to present the case that Irish social class structures are quite rigid in that they have not allowed for social mobility. He states in his article:

> What we can say is that only 1 in 20 moved from manual origins to the professional and managerial class, while a mere 2% of those with fathers in the latter class were currently in manual work. Movement from rags to riches is rarer than movement from rags to relative affluence, but a great deal more common than movement from riches to rags.

Whelan continues that it has been a characteristic of the Irish social class system that manual workers find it harder to progress through the social hierarchy than 'the intermediate non-manual class' or those born in the professional and managerial class. He goes on to examine, as will we, the reasons for this persistent lack of social mobility, the ways in which it might be alleviated and whether it has changed in any way over the last few decades.

10.5 SOCIAL MOBILITY: SOME CONTRIBUTORY FACTORS

Education is, theoretically, a strong enabler of social mobility allowing movement between social classes on the basis of acquisition of primary, secondary and third-level education. This vocational training (in areas such as medicine, commerce, science and arts) has a greater societal value, in terms of potential remuneration, than more manual and unskilled work. Accordingly, individuals who acquire this training are more likely to earn more and to attain a higher social class.

Longer periods in education with corresponding levels of instruction and qualifications gives an individual more bargaining power when competing in the marketplace. As Whelan (in Nolan & Callan, 1994) puts it:

> Education is of course the most important mechanism by which advantages associated with class origin are translated into access to desirable class locations …

and:

> … the higher one's level of education, the greater one's chances of achieving a secure and well-paid job and avoiding unemployment and poverty.

The consequences of not having these education credentials are starkly laid out by Whelan (in Nolan & Callan, 1994):

> The complete absence of educational qualifications increases the risk of exposure to poverty, both because it condemns those experiencing such failure to unskilled working-class occupations and because, within the lower working class, those without qualifications have less satisfactory labour market experiences.

Although there are state grants to encourage students from deprived backgrounds to participate in the later stages of the educational process at third level, not as many of them have done compared to those from middle class backgrounds. This is in spite of the fact that since 1967 education has been nominally free, as the then Minister for Education, Donagh O'Malley, provided free transport and free secondary schooling.

The aim was to encourage participation by those from the more deprived classes and geographical areas whose involvement in the educational system usually ended once they reached the legal age for leaving school. Early school leavers often left because they had to provide additional income for their family and because the additional expenditure on secondary, let alone third-level, education was not within the family means.

The effect of this 'free' education (it was not fully free as books, school uniforms and other unforeseen items were not included) was to increase the number of 15-year-olds still at school from less than half to over 85 per cent between 1965 and 1979. However, in the early 1980s it was still more likely that young people from a more deprived background were more likely to leave school without any qualifications. As Whelan (1985) states:

> At second level, it has been estimated that boys from upper non-manual families are at least six times more likely to sit for the Leaving Certificate than are those whose father is an unskilled or semi-skilled manual worker. Furthermore, they are almost thirteen times more likely to enter third level education.

The consequence is that those leaving school without any qualification are much more likely to be unemployed than those who leave school with a Leaving Certificate. However, increased participation alone does not necessarily increase the chance that those from deprived backgrounds will stay in the educational system longer.

Studying the effects of free second-level education between 1973 and 1987, Breen and Whelan (1996) were able to say:

> ... the advantages associated with class differences in resources have shown virtually no change, despite the continued processes of economic development and significant social change.

> One possible reason why we observe relatively little change is that the working through of policies that might be expected to influence the pattern of social fluidity—most notably, perhaps, the educational reforms of the late 1960s and early 1970s—is a long-term process. In the 1973 data almost none of the sample would have benefitted from free secondary education, while even in the 1987 data this is confined to the younger members of the sample.

There is a number of possible reasons for the difference in attitude towards education on the part of the different social classes. Middle-class parents place a greater emphasis on education; middle-class schools are less likely to have pupils with untreated educational impairments (such as reading, writing or learning difficulties) and are more likely to place a greater emphasis on educational achievement, as measured by entry to third-level colleges.

However, it may well be that poor social mobility is perpetuated by poor facilities in some secondary schools. Smyth (1999) sought to examine this difference in terms of academic and personal development of pupils in secondary schools. She says that 'pupil absenteeism and drop-out rates tend to be lower in schools which enhance academic progress among pupils.' Middle-class schools achieve more academic progress than schools with a higher working-class representation, which experience greater drop-out and absentee rates. This is due to less resourcing from central government, and the parents having less access to funding for discretionary materials and activities. This would have an effect on the school's ability to improve academic progress.

Schools with a high number of students from deprived backgrounds have to give a greater proportion of resources to deal with the fact that more of their pupils have learning difficulties, as the parents have less access to private therapeutic services and have to rely on overstretched public services with long waiting lists. More State funding at primary level may alleviate this situation, and perhaps enable more pupils from deprived backgrounds to participate further in the educational system.

While industrialisation and an upturn in the world economy in the 1960s allowed Ireland to finance the provision of a 'free' educational system, it has not led to a significant amount of social mobility. Those from less skilled and more deprived classes are more prone to unemployment owing to their lack of qualifications. They have also been traditionally more likely to emigrate.

Industrialisation has meant that Ireland's class system has stayed largely intact, with the more economically advantaged classes benefitting from the education provision. Little movement upwards has occurred from the unskilled manual classes: they are less likely to marry and their children are more likely to be the victims of infant mortality.

It might also be argued that the increased funding for education— including the abolition of fees for third-level education in the 1990s— has led to a situation where the causes of poor levels of progression in education among less advantaged socio-economic groupings will be gradually eliminated. Nevertheless, it would seem that Ireland still has a well-demarcated social-class system, and that, for some people, mobility within it is still quite difficult. As a final comment, it might be said that, irrespective of social-class background, the advances in Irish education in the last thirty years put the country in a good position to supply the companies setting up in Ireland with well-educated and trained individuals.

10.6 AGE AND DEPENDENCY

The dependency ratio is a measure of the number of people in a society who are dependent on those at work. This includes the elderly, children, students, the unemployed and those who are dependent on the state.

In 1986, Ireland had a high dependency ratio of 227 persons depending on every 100 working (Fahey and Fitzgerald, 1997). This was due to high unemployment and a large young population. It had important implications for the provision of health care, education and social services. A high dependency ratio means that there are fewer people to pay for these services and each worker has to provide for more dependent people.

Since the mid Eighties, however, the dependency ratio has fallen substantially to 188.4 dependents per 100 Irish workers in 1996, and was projected to fall to 163.5 by 2001 (Fahey and Fitzgerald, 1997).

Sweeney (1998) explains the reduction as follows:

> The ratio has fallen and will continue to fall even more rapidly in the next ten to twenty years. The forecast for 2010 … is only 125 dependants per 100 workers … and there will also be a decline in the numbers of elderly, in contrast to other European states. This reduction in dependency will greatly improve Ireland's average living standards. It was the Irish people who, around 1980, reduced the dependency by embracing contraception … and having less children.

Others reasons for a lower dependency ratio included: the two-thirds of the Irish population who were below the age of twenty in the early 1980s became older and moved into the workforce; more women came into the workforce, and an improved economic climate led to fewer people being dependent on the State.

As the Irish population gets older there will be higher dependence on the state (which is called 'old dependence' in the economic indicators) and greater pressure on state finances. To provide for this contingency, the Government established a fund, paid for by the sale of the former An Bord Telecom. The legislation that accompanied the fund's establishment mandated future governments to continue contributing regular amounts so that the State will be able to provide fully for the needs of an older population.

10.7 IRELAND'S FUTURE — MORE OF THE SAME?

Ireland's economic success story at the end of the twentieth century has been described here and elsewhere. Strong investment in Ireland from foreign companies and very good economic indicators would suggest that Ireland is well placed for the start of the twenty-first century. Yet there may be cause for concern in certain areas, some of them economic.

This argument would propose that Ireland's relative prosperity is based on previous large payments from the EU and substantial inward investment from foreign multinationals. With the exception of farm subsidies, EU funding is drying up and will almost completely disappear in the near future, as poorer EU regions claim these funds. Secondly, large multinationals located here due to a highly educated workforce, a very competitive wage-cost base and a very preferential corporation-tax system. It is quite possible that pressures on pay due to increasing affluence and the end of preferential tax rates—perhaps from European Commission pressure to suppress these—will lead to these businesses relocating to low-cost, low-taxation economies in the developing world.

Multinationals in the textiles and clothing sectors have shown willingness to move quickly out of countries on the basis of such factors. There is no reason to believe that Ireland is any different. Opponents of this argument might say that this is overly pessimistic and that Ireland has progressed into a point where it is no longer so dependent on foreign investment. Being less dependent—the argument would go—Ireland could easily recover from a number of such industries withdrawing their factories.

It remains to be seen which is the correct analysis. The final section below concludes this chapter.

10.8 CONCLUSIONS

As many commentators have stated, Ireland has moved into a more pluralist era. Divorce was passed by referendum in 1995, the fertility rates are marginally above the EU average, and fewer people see the need to be married to live together and have children. The place of the Catholic Church is less fundamental since the visit of Pope John Paul II to Ireland in 1979, when there was a brief resurgence in religious vocations and in the numbers attending the sacraments. Nevertheless, attitudes towards sexuality and the importance of the family remain similar.

In 2002, Ireland is experiencing a time of relative economic affluence, with very strong future economic indicators. This has led to a strong improvement in the previously poor dependency ratio, as the Government has to concentrate less on providing social welfare and support for a large section of the Irish population, as is the case in large European countries such as France and Germany.

In spite of this relative affluence, there is cause for concern that some less advantaged sections of society participate less in the economic life of the country. Increasing social mobility—through an improved education system—must continue to be a government priority well into the twenty-first century.

While the economic fundamentals are strong, present and future governments should be careful of the role played by foreign investment and they should foster the local elements that have led to our present success. As the Yeats quotation mentioned at the start of this chapter suggests, a terrible beauty has been born and it will be interesting to see how it grows in future years.

10.9 SUMMARY

1. Ireland has had a very distinctive pattern of emigration, because of a traditional lack of employment prospects. Since the early 1990s, Ireland has experienced net immigration due to returning emigrants and immigrating EU and non-EU nationals.

2. The present Irish pattern of migration, similar to other European countries, has emerged since the increasing industrialisation of the State began in the early 1950s. Fewer people are employed in the agricultural sector, and many more in industry. This has resulted in people moving to the east of the country, which has now approximately 30 per cent of the country's population.

3. Ireland's pattern of fertility and nuptiality now matches more closely the European norm: fewer people get married and the fertility rate conforms more to the EU average.

4. Ireland has fairly rigid and structured class system that permits poor levels of social mobility.

5. Ireland's dependency ratio, in contrast to some of its European counterparts, has fallen from a previous high level as unemployment has decreased and more of its young population has come into the workforce.

10.10 EXAM QUESTIONS

1. Examine the level of social mobility in Ireland, with particular reference to the factors contributing to its existence. (Institute of Technology Tallaght, 1998)

2. What has been the impact on marketing practice of the changes in Irish demography over the last twenty years? (MII, 1998)

3. Discuss the main changes in Irish demography over the last forty years, stating the reasons why such changes have occurred. (MII, 1997)

4. Describe the changes that have taken place in Irish demography and population over the last forty years. Analyse the reasons for

10.10 EXAM QUESTIONS CONTD.

these changes, and suggest how you think Ireland's demography and population will develop in future years. (Institute of Technology Tallaght, 2001)

5. Analyse the importance to Irish society of the family. Trace its influence in the last fifty years and explain how and why it has changed. (Institute of Technology Tallaght, 2001)

REFERENCES

CHAPTER 1

Allport, G. (1947), *The Use of Personal Documents in Psychological Science*, New York: Social Science Research Council.

Boring, E.G. in Schultz, D. (1982), *A History of Modern Psychology* (3rd edition), New York: Academic Press.

Chisnall, P. (1985), *Marketing: A Behavioural Analysis* (2nd edition), Maidenhead: McGraw-Hill.

Coon, D. (1987), *Introduction to Psychology: Exploration and Application* (4th edition), St.Paul: West Publishing.

Francis, A. (1988), *Business Mathematics and Statistics*, Hampshire: DP Publications.

Hair, J. F., Jr., Anderson, R.E., Tatham, R.L., & Black, W.C. (1992), *Multivariate Data Analysis*, New York: Maxwell MacMillan.

James, Henry, (1890), *The Science of Mental Life*, Boston: Harvard University Press.

Kahreman and Tversky (1973) in Schultz, D. (1985), *A History of Modern Psychology* (3rd edition), New York: Academic Press.

CHAPTER 2

Best, J.B. (1986), *Cognitive Psychology*, St. Paul: West Publishing.

Kelley, H.H. (1980) in B. Weiner (ed.), *Human Motivation*, New York: Holt, Rinehart and Winston.

Kretch, D., Crutchfield, R.S. and Ballachey, E.L. (1962), *Individual in Society*, New York: McGraw Hill.

Langer, E.J. and Abelson, R.P. (1974), 'A patient by any other name. Clinician Group Differences in Labelling Bias', *Journal of Consulting and Clinical Psychology*, 42, 4-9.

Logothetis, N.K. (1999), 'Vision: a Window on Consciousness', *Scientific American*, November.

Rothbart, M and Birrell, P. (1977), 'Attitude and the Perception of Faces', *Journal of Research Personality*, 11, 209-215.

Webster (1982), 'Decision-making in the Employment Interview', in Mikell, T.R. and Larson J.R. (eds.) (1987), *People in Organisations*, New York: McGraw Hill.

CHAPTER 3

Atkinson, R.C. & Shiffrin, R.M. (1971). 'The Control of Short Term Memory', *Scientific American*, 224.

Coon, D. (1986), *Introduction to Psychology*, St. Paul: West Publishing.

Hicks, D. (Ed.) (1996), *Discourse, learning and schooling*, Cambridge: Cambridge University Press.

Kohler, W. (1925), *The Mentality of Apes*, New York: Harcourt Brace.

Millar, G. (1956), 'Learning' in *Introductory Psychology: An Experimental Approach*, Wright, D. & Taylor, A. (1978), UK: Penguin Education.

Pavlov, I.P. (1927), *Conditioned Reflexes*, London: Oxford University Press.

Skinner, B.F. (*1953*), *Science and Human Behaviour*, New York: MacMillan.

Tolman, E.C. (1939), *Purposive Behaviour in Animals and Men*, New York: Appleton-Century-Crofts.

CHAPTER 4

Adams, J.S., (1965). 'Injustice in Social Exchange' in Berkowitz, L. (ed.), *Advances in Experimental Social Psychology*, New York: Academic Press.

Arnold, J., Cooper, C. and Robertson, I.T. (1998), *Work Psychology: Understanding Human Behaviour in the Workplace* (3rd ed.), London: Pitman.

Buchanan, D. & Huczynski, A. (1991), *Organizational Behaviour*, London: Prentice Hall.

Galbraith, J. & Cummings L.L, 'An Empirical Investigation of the Motivational Determinants of Task Performance', *Organizational Behaviour and Human Performance*, vol. 2, 1967, 237-257.

Herzberg, F. *et al.*, (1959), *The Motivation to Work*, New York: Wiley.

Maslow, A.H., *Toward a Psychology of Being* (2nd ed.), Princeton, NJ: D. Van Nostrand, 1968.

McClelland, D.C., *The Achieving Society*, New York: Free Press, 1961.

McGregor, D., (1960), *The Human Side of Enterprise*, New York McGraw Hill.

Taylor, F.W. (1947), *Scientific Management*, New York: Harper & Row.

Vroom, V.H., (1964), *Work and Motivation*, New York: Wiley.

Vroom, V.H. and Deci, E.L. (1970), *Management and Motivation* Harmondsworth: Penguin.

CHAPTER 5

Allport, G.W. (1954), *The Nature of Prejudice*, Reading, Massachusetts: Addison-Wesley.

Bogardus, E.S. (1925). 'Measuring Social Distance', *Journal of Applied Sociology*, 9, 299-308.

Eagly, A.H. and Chaiken, S. (1993), *The Psychology of Attitudes*, San Diego, CA: Harcourt Brace Jovanovich.

Festinger, L. (1967), *A Theory of Cognitive Dissonance*, New York: Harper & Row.

Fishbein, L. (1957), 'Attitudes and Prediction of Behaviour' in M. Fishbein (ed.), *Attitudes, Theory and Measurement*, New York: Wiley.

Fishbein, M. & Azjen, I. (1975), *Belief, Attitude, Intention and Behaviour*, Reading, Mass.: Addison-Wesley.

Katz, D. (1960), 'The Functional Approach to the Study of Attitudes', *Public Opinion Quarterly*, 24, 163-204.

Kretch, D., Crutchfield, R.S. and Ballachey, E.L. (1962), *The Individual in Society*, New York: McGraw Hill.

Likert, R. (1932), 'A Technique for the Measurement of Attitudes', *Archives of Psychology*, 22, 140.

Loudon, D.L. & Della Bitta, A.J. (1993), *Consumer Behaviour: Concepts and Applications*, New York: McGraw Hill.

Osgood, C.E., Suci, G.J. & Tannenbaum, P.H. (1957), *The Measurement of Meaning*, Urbana, Illinois: University of Illinois Press.

Thurstone, L.L. & Chave, E.J. (1929), *Primary Mental Attitudes*, Chicago: University of Chicago Press.

CHAPTER 6

Cattell, R.B., *Structured Personality-Learning Theory*, New York: Praeger, 1983.

Dworetzky, J.P. (1985), Psychology. (2nd ed.), St. Paul, MN: West.

Eysenck, M. (ed.) (1998), *Psychology: Anintegrated Approach*, London: Longman.

Freud, S. *New Introductory Lectures on Psychoanalysis* in standard edition (Vol. 22), London: Hogarth Press, 1964. (First German edition, 1933) (a).

Gross, R.D. (1992), Psychology: *The Science of Mind and Behaviour*, London: Hodder and Stoughton.

Jung, C.G., 'Psychological Types' in *Collected Works* (Vol. 6), Princeton, NJ: Princeton University Press, 1971. (First German edition, 1921).

Rogers, C.R., (1961), *On Becoming a Person*, Boston: Houghton Mifflin.

Rogers, C.R., (1959), 'A Theory of Therapy, Personality and Inter-personal Relationships as Developed in the Client-centered Framework', in S. Koch (ed.), *Psychology: A Study of Science* (vol. 3), New York: McGraw-Hill.

CHAPTER 7

Asch, S. (1956), 'Studies of Independence and Conformity', in R.M. Steers, *Introduction to Organisational Behaviour* (1991), New York: Harper Collins.

Huczynski, A and Buchanan, D. (2001), *Organisational Behaviour: An Introductory Text* (4th ed.), London: Financial Times-Prentice Hall.

Festinger, L. (1950), 'Informal Social Communication', *Psychological Review,* (1983) Sept. p. 275.

Furnham, A. (1997), *The Psychology of Behaviour at Work: The Individual in the Organization*, Hove: Psychology Press.

Gaylin, W. (1984), *The Rage Within*, New York: Simon & Schuster.

Hackman, J and Morris, C., 'Group Tasks, Group Interaction Process and Group Performance Effectiveness', in L. Berkowitz (ed.) (1975), *Advances in Experimental Social Psychology.* (vol. 8), New York: Academic Press.

Hall, G. and Lindzey, G. (1985), *Introduction to Theories of Personality*, New York: John Wiley.

Kiesler, C.A. and Kiesler, S.B. (1969), 'Conformity' in D. Myers, *Social Psychology* (1990), New York: McGraw-Hill.

Loudon, D. and Della Bitta, G. (1993), *Consumer Behaviour: Concepts and Applications*, New York: McGraw-Hill.

Milgram, S. (1974), *Obedience to Authority*, New York: Harper and Row.

Morris, W. and Miller, R. S. (1975), 'The Effect of Consensus-breaking and Consensus-pre-empting Partners on Reduction of Conformity' in D.G. Myers (1990), *Social Psychology*, New York: McGraw-Hill.

Moorhead, G. and Griffen, R. (1992), *Organisational Behaviour* (3rd ed.), MA: Houghton Griffin.

Mullen, B. (1985), 'Strength and Immediacy of Sources', *Journal of Personality and Social Psychology*, 48, 1458-1466.

Sherif, M. and Sherif, C. (1969), *Social Psychology*, New York: Harper and Row.

Tuckman, B and Jenson, M., 'Stages of Small Group Development

Revisited', *Groups and Organisational Studies*, 1977, 2, 419-442.

Tuckman, B. (1965), 'Development Sequences in Small Groups', *Psychological Bulletin*, 63, 384-399.

CHAPTER 8

Davis, K and Newstrom, J. (1985), *Human Behaviour at Work: Organisational Behaviour* (7th ed.), New York : McGraw-Hill.

Katz, D. and Kahn, R.L. (1978), *The Social Psychology of Organisations* (2nd ed.), New York : Liviley.

Morgan, G. (1997), *Images of Organization*, (2nd ed.), Thousand Oaks, CA: Sage.

Moorhead and Griffen (1992), *Organisational Behaviour*, (3rd ed.), Boston : Houghton Miffin.

Nicholas, R. (1962), 'Listening is Good Business' in Steers, R. (1993), *Introduction to Organisational Behavioural*, New York: Harper Collins.

O'Reilly, C. and Pondy, L.R., 'Organisational Communication' in Moorhead and Griffen (1989), *Organisation Behaviour*, (3rd ed.), Boston: Houghton Miffin.

Schein, E. F. (1985), *Organisational Change and Leadership*, San Francisco: Jossey Bass.

Snyder, R. and Morris, J. (1984), 'Organisational Communication and Performance', *Journal of Applied Psychology*, August.

Trist, E. and Banforth, K. (1951), 'Some Social and Psychological Consequences of the Long-wall Method of Coal Getting', *Human Relations*, February 1951.

CHAPTER 9

Fanning, R. (1983, *Independent Ireland*, Dublin: Criterion Press.

Kluckhohn, C. in Loudon, D. & Della Biutta, A. (1993). *Consumer Behaviour: Concepts & Applications*, New York: McGraw Hill.

Piaget, J. (1966), *The Psychology of Intelligence*, Towota, NJ: Littlefield, Adams.

Shiffman, L. & Kanuck, L. (1997), *Consumer Behaviour* (3rd ed.), Upper Saddle River: NJ.

Yussen S. & Santrock, J.C 1987), *Child Development: An Introduction*, Iowa: W.C. Brown. New Jersey: Prentice Hall.

CHAPTER 10

Breen, R. and Whelan, C.T. (1996), *Social Mobility and Social Class in Ireland*, Dublin: Gill & Macmillan.

Breen, R., Hannan, D.F., Rottman, D.B. and Whelan, C.T. (1990), *Understanding Contemporary Ireland*, Dublin: Gill and Macmillan.

Central Statistics Office (2001), *Regional Population Projections: 2001-2031*. Dublin: CSO (www.cso.ie).

Dillon, M. (1998), 'Divorce and Cultural Rationality' in M. Peillon and E. Slater (ed.s) *Encounters with Modern Ireland*, Dublin: Institute of Public Administration.

Fahey, T. & Fitz Gerald, J. (1997), *Welfare Implications of Demographic Trends*, Dublin: Oak Tree Press.

Fanning, R. (1983), *Independent Ireland*, Dublin: Helican Ltd.

Foley, E. (1998), *The Irish Market–A Profile*, Dublin: The Marketing Institute.

Greer, G. (1967), *The Female Eunuch*, London: Pan.

Kennedy, F. (2001), *From Cradle to Crèche*, Dublin: Institute of Public Administration.

Kennedy, F. (1986). 'The Family in Transition' in K.A. Kennedy (ed.) *Ireland in Transition: Economic and Social Change*, Dublin: Mercier.

Kennedy, K., Giblin, T. and McHugh, D. (1988), *The Economic Development of Ireland in the Twentieth Century*, London: Routledge.

Labour Force Survey (1996), Dublin: Stationery Office.

Labour Force Survey (1986), Dublin: Stationery Office.

MacDonagh, J. & Weldridge, R. (1994), *Behavioural Science for Marketing and Business Students*, Dublin: Gill & Macmillan.

Rottman, D. and O'Connell, P.J. (1982) 'The Changing Social Structure of Ireland' in F. Litton (ed.), *Unequal Achievement: The Irish Experience 1957-1982*, Dublin: Institute of Public Administration.

Smyth, E. (1999), *Do Schools Differ?*, Dublin: Oak Tree Press.

Sweeney, P. (1998), *The Celtic Tiger: Ireland's Economic Miracle Explained*, Dublin: Oak Tree Press.

Tansey, P. (1998), *Ireland at Work*, Dublin: Oak Tree Press.

Whelan, C.T. (1994), 'Poverty, Social Class, Education and Intergenerational Mobility' in B.Nolan & T.Callan (ed.s), *Poverty Policy in Ireland*, Dublin: Gill & Macmillan.

Whelan, C.T. (1994), 'Irish Social Values: Traditional or Modern?' in C.T. Whelan (ed.), *Values and Social Change in Ireland*, Dublin: Gill & Macmillan.

Whelan, C.T. & Fahey, T. (1994), *Marriage and the Family*, in C.T. Whelan (ed.), *Values and Social Change in Ireland*, Dublin: Gill & Macmillan.

Whelan, C.T. and Whelan, B.J. (1985), 'Equality of Opportunity in Irish Schools: A Reassessment', *Economic and Social Review*, 16, (2), 103-114.